Contents

Teacher's introduction

About the book

PET Preparation and Practice introduces students to the Preliminary English Test, helps to develop the skills required to pass, and provides students with opportunities to assess their progress through practice test questions. There is comprehensive coverage of the functions, grammar, topics and vocabulary listed in the syllabus.

The *With Answers* edition contains a full answer key, including sample answers for Writing questions and the transcript of all the recorded material.

Organization

The structure of the book follows the order of questions in the exam: Reading, Parts 1–5; Writing, Parts 1–3; Listening, Parts 1–4; and Speaking, Parts 1–4. Each question is taken in turn and starts with a clear explanation of what is being tested. The Preparation exercises which follow the explanation develop student awareness of the tasks involved and give guidance on how to answer the question. After the Preparation exercises there is a Test practice question. At the end of each skill section there is a test of all the questions in that skill. There is a complete test on pages 95–107, following the Speaking section.

How and when to use the book

PET Preparation and Practice can be integrated into a general language course to introduce students to the exam gradually and develop their exam skills over the duration of the course. Alternatively, the book can be used for intensive exam preparation at the end of a general course, or as a short exam course in itself.

The exam questions can be approached in any order. It is recommended that a minimum of one Preparation section (e.g. Writing, Part 1 pages 38–44) is completed at one time. There is a key to the Preparation exercises and Test questions in the *With Answers* edition. The recorded material includes input for the Preparation sections to some questions in the Reading, Writing, and Speaking sections, in addition to Preparation and Test practice for the Listening part of the exam. The Listening test questions include recorded instructions as in the exam.

The test questions

There are three practice tests in the book; two are integrated with the preparation work, and one appears in full at the end of the book.

1 The first test is divided up into single questions and occurs immediately after the Preparation section for each question, for example, Test practice, Part 1 on page 13. This gives students the opportunity to try out the skills presented and practised through the preceding Preparation exercises. There is no need to set a time limit on the Test practice at this stage, although it is advisable to go over these initial Test practice questions thoroughly in class, referring back when necessary to the explanations and Preparation exercises.

2 The second test appears at the end of each skill section, for example, Reading test, pages 32–37. After students have completed the Preparation and Test practice for all the exam questions in one area, they can attempt the practice test in that skill. It would be helpful to time these tests: 45 minutes each for reading and writing; 30 minutes for listening. The timing for the Speaking test can be more flexible, depending on how the speaking practice is set up (see suggestions below).

3 The third test appears in full on pages 95–107. Students can do this test after they have studied all the Preparation exercises and attempted the separate skill tests. This test should be completed, as far as possible, under exam conditions. Students should be seated at separate desks, without class books and without a dictionary. There should be no talking, and the time allowed to complete the paper should be two hours for reading, writing and listening.

Using the answer sheets

In spring 1994 answer sheets were introduced for the PET. This means that candidates no longer write their answers on the test paper itself, but mark up an answer sheet, by filling in lozenges or writing their answers out. For Parts 1–3 (Writing) students may use the test paper for their rough work, but must transfer their answers to the answer sheet. For the Listening test, 12 minutes will be given at the end of the test for candidates to transfer their answers to the answer sheet. Examples of the answer sheets are given on pages 108–110. These are photocopiable and can be used with any of the test questions.

The introduction of the answer sheets has meant that some of the questions in the test have been modified to standardize the number of items. All the test questions in this book reflect these changes, including consecutive numbering of items throughout the main sections of the test.

Practising the Speaking test

Examination conditions are difficult to reproduce for this part of the test. During the preparation for the exam, try to arrange for students to be in an interview with a teacher. If this is not possible students can work in pairs to the guidelines given in each task. Students should be able to show that they have something to say about the topics raised in this area of the examination and respond to tasks in the role play. It may help after the Speaking Test practice to ask students to assess their own or their partners' performances, using the framework suggested in the marking scheme. If a student can keep a conversation going with a partner, can communicate ideas successfully, and is able to paraphrase, he or she is on the way to success in the exam.

When students are all working together on the Speaking test in the same room, and all speaking at the same time, it will still be possible to monitor their performance to some extent. Look out for signs of failure to communicate, students who fall silent or give answers that are too brief. For a more detailed assessment refer to the marking scheme.

Marking the test questions

The marking procedures below provide guidance in awarding marks for the PET. There is an answer key to the questions on pages 113–125 of the *With Answers* edition. The key includes sample answers for written questions. These are a general guide to what is expected; a student may, of course, produce something quite different from the sample, but which would be equally acceptable.

READING
Part 1 Each correct answer receives 1 mark. Possible total of 5 marks.

Part 2 Each correct answer receives 1 mark. Possible total of 5 marks.

Part 3 Correct answers receive 1 mark. Possible total of 5 marks.

Part 4 Correct answers receive 1 mark. Possible total of 10 marks.

Part 5 Correct answers receive 1 mark. Possible total of 10 marks.

Scaling
The four sections of the Preliminary English Test – Reading, Writing, Listening and Speaking – each carry 25% of the total marks. However, the marks for the Reading section do not add up to 25. In this case the raw mark is scaled by computer so that it represents 25% of the total mark.

WRITING
Part 1 The marking for Part 1 is quite strict. Each new sentence should have the correct grammar, vocabulary and spelling to receive a full mark. No half marks are given. Total of 5 marks.

Part 2 There is 1 mark for each of the 10 questions. Content and language are both taken into account. The part of the answer that contains the key information should be error-free. Total of 10 marks.

Part 3 A total of 10 marks is available for Part 3: 5 marks to cover the content and completion of task, and 5 marks to cover the language used. To be given full marks, an answer should contain suitable and coherent content, convey the correct tone for the task set, show an appropriate range of vocabulary and structures and give a general impression of accuracy.

LISTENING
Part 1 Each correct answer receives 1 mark. Total of 7 marks.

Part 2 Each correct answer receives 1 mark. Total of 6 marks.

Part 3 Each correct answer receives 1 mark. Total of 6 marks.

Part 4 Each correctly ticked box receives 1 mark. Total of 6 marks.

SPEAKING ASSESSMENT
The Speaking Test is taken by candidates in pairs with two examiners. One of these examiners, the interlocutor, takes part in the interaction, while the other (the assessor) does not.

Both examiners award marks. The assessor takes the following elements into consideration when giving marks:
- grammar and vocabulary   • pronunciation
- discourse management   • interactive communication

The marks for each of these four elements are on a scale of 0–5. The top 4–5 band, for example, indicates that a speaker is able to convey a message in a familiar situation with relative ease (minor errors which do not obscure meaning may still be present) and that he/she can find the words needed to communicate the intended message, using paraphrase if necessary; that he/she can express himself or herself coherently and effectively; that pronunciation is clear enough to be understood despite a recognizable L1 influence; and that he/she can take part in the interaction by initiating and responding appropriately and at a natural speed.

The interlocutor gives a general impression mark. The total mark is scaled to represent 25% of the overall marks for the PET.

Student's introduction

What is the Preliminary English Test?

The PET tests your ability to understand English when you read and listen, and your ability to communicate when you speak and write English. The PET is for students at intermediate level.

The first part of the test includes the Reading and Writing sections. You have to show in the test that you can deal with everyday situations, using English to make yourself understood. You have to read signs, to understand short reading passages, to find the information you need when you are reading, and to understand why the writer has written the passage. In the Writing section you should be able to write about things that happen, and about people and places. You will also have to write about your feelings. The Reading and Writing part of the test lasts one and a half hours in total.

In the Listening test you have to be able to understand short announcements, and to get the information you need from a longer speech. You will also have to answer questions about a conversation between two people. The Listening test lasts thirty minutes.

In the Speaking test you should be able to answer questions about yourself in English, ask another student questions and share ideas, and describe pictures and say what you think of them.

What does this book do?

This book will tell you about the questions in the PET. It will show you how to prepare for and answer the questions so that you do not waste time and so that you can show the examiners what you can do. There are also Test practice questions for you to practise the exam skills you are learning.

The *With Answers* edition contains an answer key, including sample answers for the Writing questions and the transcript of all the recorded material.

How to use this book on your own

You can do the Preparation sections in any order you like. The book starts with the Reading section and goes on to the Writing, Listening and Speaking sections, in the order they appear in the test. Do all the work on one question of the test at the same time. For example, in the Writing section, Part 1, work through the Preparation exercises 1–7 on pages 38–43, checking your answers in the key, page 116. When you have completed the Preparation exercises, try the Test practice question. After you have done the Test practice question check your answer with the key, page 116. If your answer is incorrect, look at the test question again and work out where you went wrong. If you made a lot of mistakes, go back to the Preparation section and work through it again.

You will notice that some exercises in the book have this symbol (🖭) to show you when you should use the cassette. Listen carefully to the cassette, there will be instructions to tell you what to do.

When you check your answers to the Writing Test practice questions compare your answers with the samples in the key. Your answers will probably not be exactly the same as the samples. However, they should be about the same length and use some of the same words. Make a note of any expressions that you want to learn and use later.

Practise the Speaking section with a friend, if possible, or record some answers on a tape recorder and listen to them. Practise speaking out loud and try to make complete sentences.

Using the answer sheets

You will have to write your answers for the PET on answer sheets which will be given out with the test papers at the beginning of the test. On pages 108–110 of this book there are examples of these answer sheets. You can make photocopies of these pages and use them when you do the Test practice questions.

P E T overview

PAPER 1 | Time: 1½ hours

Reading
PARTS

1

2

3

4

5

Writing
PARTS

1

2

3

PAPER 2 | Time: 30 minutes

Listening
PARTS

1

2

3

4

SPEAKING TEST
Time: 10–12 minutes

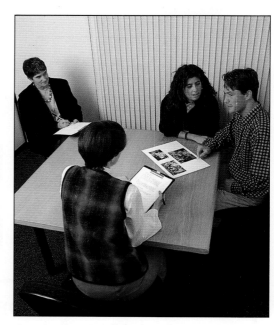

There is a full explanation of each part at the beginning of each Preparation section.

Reading

PART 1

Explanation   Part 1 tests your understanding of public notices written in English. There are five photographs, numbered one to five. Each photograph shows a public notice or sign with several words on it. Next to each photograph there are four short sentences (**A**, **B**, **C** and **D**). You must choose the sentence which explains what the words on the notice mean. When you have done this mark the correct letter on your answer sheet.

Preparation   ### Exercise 1

Look at the signs (1–30). Where would you be most likely to find them?

EXAMPLE

a   outside a cage in a zoo *14*
b   in a clothes shop window
c   on a bus, near the driver's seat
d   in the street, near some builders working on a roof

e   at the entrance to a club
f   at the start of a narrow path
g   in front of a wall which has recently been painted

1

2

NO CYCLING ON THE PATH

3

Keep off the grass

4

WET PAINT

5

Exam in progress. Do not disturb.

6

No entrance for visitors
___
Please use side door

7

SORRY
We are closed for repairs.
Reopening March 1st.

8

No admittance without a ticket

9

PRIVATE ROAD
No cars

10

TO PREVENT ACCIDENTS, PLEASE KEEP THIS GATE CLOSED

11

EXIT ONLY

12

OPEN
from 9.00 am every day

13

STAFF ENTRANCE

14

Please don't feed the animals

15

NO SMOKING

16

NO PARKING
Keep this space clear

17

Don't eat in this area

18

Members only

19

— WARNING —
Dangerous Machinery.
Please keep this gate closed.

20

Please do not touch.
All breakages must be paid for.

21

STUDENT RATES AVAILABLE
Ask the receptionist for details

22

WARNING

Staff only
beyond
this point

23

PLEASE RING FOR ASSISTANCE AND THEN WAIT.

24

PLEASE DO NOT TALK TO THE DRIVER

25

All parcels must be left at the desk

26

TICKETS AVAILABLE
from the desk at reception
after 6.00 pm

27

Last show starts at 8.30

28

LOW CEILING
Please mind your head

29

Final reductions
All leather jackets
15% off

30

Emergency exit Keep clear

Now look at the table below. Where do you think you would see signs with these key words or phrases? Work in pairs to complete the table.

Key phrases	indoors	outdoors	a shop	a road	a public office	public transport	a place of work	a place of entertainment
sale	✓	✓	✓					
parking		✓		✓				
no entry								
side door								
last show								
reductions								
passengers								
entrance								
exit								
all breakages must be paid for								
staff entrance								
drive on left								
vehicle								

Exercise 2

There are four different kinds of signs:
- *information* signs tell you what to do (for example, *ENTRANCE*)
- *prohibition* signs tell you not to do something (for example, *NO SMOKING*)
- *warning* signs tell you about dangers (for example, *DANGER!*)
- *instruction* signs tell you to do something (for example, *PLEASE RING FOR SERVICE*).

Look at these key words and phrases and decide which kind of sign you would see them on. Then complete the table.

Please ...	Warning	dangerous	reductions
No ...ing	Keep off	entrance	exit
Don't ...	Please don't ...	open	closed
private	... only	... per cent off	
mind ...	Danger	on sale	

information	prohibition	warning	instruction
		Warning	*Please*

Exercise 3

Look at the signs in Exercise 1. Decide which category each sign belongs to and write the number of the sign in the table. Some signs belong to more than one category.

information	prohibition	warning	instruction
[1]	*[2]*	*[1]*	

Exercise 4

Look at the signs in Exercise 1. Which ones mean the same as these sentences? Write the numbers of the signs. Sometimes more than one answer is possible.

a   You must not walk on the grass.   .....
b   If you break anything you must pay for it.   .....
c   You can't go in here unless you are a member of staff.   .....
d   You must not make a noise in this place, because some people are taking an examination.   .....
e   You need a ticket to go in here.   .....
f   If you need help, you should first ring a bell and then someone will come and help you.   .....

Exercise 5

Look at each sign below and read the sentences next to it. Only one sentence is completely correct (but the others may be partly correct). Work in pairs to discuss the sentences, then decide which answer is correct. Say why the other sentences are not correct.

EXAMPLE

> **SORRY**
> We are closed for repairs.
> Reopening March 1st.

A Repair work will begin on March 1st.
   Incorrect the sign tells you that repairs are going on now. This place will open again [reopen] on March 1st.

B Repairs have been taking place here since March 1st.
   Incorrect we don't know when the repairs started, but they will finish before March 1st.

C Repairs are being carried out until March 1st.
   Correct.

1

> Last show starts at 8.30

A The performance will last eight and a half hours.

B The last performance begins at half past eight.

C To see the show you must go to the theatre after 8.30.

2

> —— **WARNING** ——
> Dangerous Machinery.
> Please keep this gate closed.

A The machinery might be stolen if the gate is not kept shut.

B The gate is operated by machinery, which is dangerous.

C You must close the gate, because the machinery inside is dangerous.

3

> **TICKETS AVAILABLE**
> **from the desk at reception**
> **after 6.00 pm**

A You can collect tickets after six o'clock from the desk in reception.

B The desk in reception is closed until six o'clock.

C You can get tickets from the desk at reception, which is open until six o'clock.

4

> **All parcels**
> **must be left**
> **at the desk**

A Parcels must be taken past the desk into the building.

B If you bring a parcel into the building, leave it at the desk.

C If you are collecting a parcel, go to the desk on the left.

Test practice   **Part 1 Questions 1–5** Look at the five pictures of signs below. Someone asks
you what each sign means. For each sign mark the correct letter – **A**, **B**, **C** or **D** –
on your answer sheet.

Example:

Part 1				
O	A	B	C	D
	■	☐	☐	☐

1.

A Employees of the café are allowed to put their cars here.

B People using the café can park here, but nobody else can.

C Nobody is allowed to park in front of the café.

D People can park here if they pay a parking fee.

2.

A You can't use this subway to cross the road.

B There is no entrance to the subway on this side of the road.

C If you want to cross the road, you must use the subway.

D If you want to use the subway you must cross the road.

3.

A The shop opens at 9.00 every day.

B The shop is only open on Sundays.

C The shop opens at 5.30 on Sundays.

D The shop is closed on Sundays.

4.

A You can walk on the path but you may not ride a bicycle.

B Only members of the public can cycle on the path.

C The path is closed except for cyclists.

D People are allowed to walk and ride bicycles on this path.

5.

A You can't go into this building because it is being repaired.

B You may not go through this door because building work is going on.

C The other door has not been built yet.

D Builders must deliver their materials at the other door.

PART 2

Explanation   Part 2 contains eight texts (**A–H**), 300–400 words in total. They could be from advertisements, public notices, or information sheets. This question tests how well you can look through short texts to find particular pieces of information. You must look through the texts and match the correct information to the questions. It is not necessary to read or understand everything in the texts. When you write your answers you must mark the correct letter – **A** to **H** – on your answer sheet.

Preparation   ## Exercise 1

Read this list of presents you need to buy for people. Then fill in as much information as you can in the table. If you cannot find the information, leave the box empty.

1 something to wear for cousin Mary (aged twenty), costing less than £12 – something useful
2 something small for mother to carry in her handbag
3 a game for Michael to play with his friends
4 a musical instrument for John (aged thirty), suitable for a beginner
5 a vase for grandmother which will hold flowers

	1	2	3	4	5
type of article	*clothing*				
for a man/woman/child	*woman*				
price	*less than £12*				
anything else	*something useful*				

Exercise 2

Look at this page from a catalogue. Quickly scan the page for information about the size of the things for sale. Match the measurements (1–5) with the things they refer to, e.g. 54″ *shoulder bag strap*

1 13″ long   2 2″ in diameter   3 6″ in diameter   4 42″ chest   5 3¾″ high

Exercise 3

Now scan the same catalogue page and find which items are made from these materials, e.g. soft handspun wool *mountain jumper*

1 local clay   2 the bark of the 'Bita' tree   3 real leather   4 local wood   5 copper

EMBROIDERED MONEY BELT

This Thai money belt has stylised chicken's feet embroidery in blue, white, green and pink. It will fit up to a 32" waist, has a security catch and would make an excellent present for anybody involved in outdoor pursuits.
23558 **£6.45**

TRINKET POT

This excellent copper pot for your earrings or brooches is made in a small workshop in Chile. The top and sides are enamelled to give it a tough long lasting surface. The pot is 1" high and 2" in diameter.
71617 **£5.95**

KEPIS LEATHER SHOULDER BAG

When we first made contact with the Indonesian producer group that makes this bag it was on the verge of collapse. Now, 6 people enjoy much better wages and conditions, and you can enjoy a real leather, handstitched shoulder bag with a big central compartment. The bag measures 9½" x 8" x 4" and the strap measures 54".
27880 **£33.95**

CERAMIC VASE

Made in local clay from the area around Masaya, Nicaragua, this vase is handpainted in natural colours to an ancient pre-Columbian design. It's 5½" high, 6" in diameter and would make a handsome vase for a dry flower display as this Nicaraguan pottery does not hold water.
70572 **£15.45**

MOUNTAIN JUMPER

Knitted by Aymara indians in Bolivia in their own homes, soft handspun wool makes this jumper a dream to wear. In blue, grey, purple and pink, it comes in one size that will fit up to 42" chest. Handwash only.
24775 **£79.50**

COIN BOX

Measuring 3" square x 1½" deep this coin box from Bangladesh folds flat when empty – then expands to take a large handful of change. The leather body is decorated with needlepoint. Colours may vary slightly.
26905 **£2.95**

BOLIVIAN FLUTE

Known as a 'Tarka' in Bolivia, this flute works in the same way as a recorder, so it's suitable for anyone just beginning to play. It is handcarved from local wood in the Highlands of Bolivia and is 13" long.
40770 **£8.45**

RING OF MUSICIANS

This charming statuette of five musicians in straw hats and bare feet show them playing everything from pan pipes to recorders. It comes from family workshops in and around Ayacucho where this traditional Peruvian ceramic folk art is produced. 3½" dia. x 3¾" high.
65820 **£5.45**

UBO CARDS

This simple to learn game of chance for two or more is named after the Filipino tribe that originated it. The cards are made from the bark of the 'Bita' tree and having played it ourselves we think you will find it most intriguing. Full instructions are supplied.
41742 **£4.25**

Exercise 4

Scan the catalogue page again and find which items were made in these countries, e.g. Bolivia *Bolivian flute, mountain jumper*

1 Chile   2 The Philippines   3 Nicaragua   4 Peru   5 Indonesia

Exercise 5

Now look back at the shopping list of presents in Exercise 1 and decide which item you would buy from the catalogue for each person.

Exercise 6

Look at all the advertisements for a few seconds to find out what they are about. Then look at questions 1–5 and quickly read the advertisements again to find the answers.

A Friendly young person wanted for evening work (six evenings per week) in busy bar. Phone 87904 for details.	**B** Lady wanted for cleaning. Three mornings per week. Must be able to work alone. Tel: 44962	**C** Driver, male or female, needed for evening work. No weekends. Please ring 23407.
D Lady with experience of children wanted to look after two small boys, 8.30 – 4.00 Mon to Fri. Phone 42356 after 6.00 p.m.	**E** Cook wanted for small country restaurant. Evenings and all day at weekends. Tel: 54328	**F** **Gardener needed one morning per week.** **Tel: 81164**
G Keen young person with driving licence needed for pizza delivery. Six evenings per week. Please ring 712087	**H** Assistant wanted to help with children's club at town museum, weekends only. Experience of working with children necessary; some knowledge of history useful. Tel 486109	

1   Do the advertisers say whether they want men or women for the jobs?

2   Do the advertisements say what times people are needed to work?

3   Do the advertisements say what age the people applying should be?

4   Do they mention any specific skills?

5   Do they mention any academic qualifications?

Exercise 7

Five people are looking for a job. Look at the information about them, then read the advertisements again and ask and answer questions a–e for each person. The first one, Greg, has been done for you.

Greg is a student, aged nineteen. He likes meeting people. He is not free during the day. He can't cook or drive a car.

Peter is sixty-five. He would like to work out of doors. He would prefer not to work in the evenings.

Jenny is forty. She does not like children. She can cook and drive, but she isn't available for work at weekends, or in the mornings.

Audrey does not want to work at weekends. She is a good cook but she can't drive. She has two children, now grown up. She wants to work indoors, but she doesn't like housework much.

Gary, aged thirty, likes cooking and gardening. He wants to work as many hours a week as possible and would prefer to work all day on Saturdays and Sundays. He has never worked with children.

EXAMPLE

a Male or Female?
   Are there any jobs Greg cannot do because he is a male? Yes, B and D.
b Hours of work?
   Are there any jobs he cannot do because he is not free during the day? Yes, B, D and F.
c Skills/preferences?
   Are there any jobs he cannot do because he cannot cook or drive? Yes, C, E and G.
   Are there any jobs Greg does not want to do? No.
d Age?
   Are there any jobs he cannot do because he is the wrong age? No.
e Which is the most suitable job for Greg? *A.*

Now write your answers in the table below by putting a cross (✗) if the person cannot do the job, and a tick (✓) if they can.

People	Jobs							
	A	B	C	D	E	F	G	H
1 Greg	✓	✗	✗	✗	✗	✗	✗	✗
2 Peter								
3 Jenny								
4 Audrey								
5 Gary								

Test practice   **Part 2 Questions 6–10** The following people want to attend evening classes. Look at the information about evening classes for the autumn term. Decide which class would be the most suitable for each person. Mark the correct letter – **A** to **H** – on the answer sheet.

Example:

6.   Jane Brown is a housewife. She is not interested in getting a qualification, but wants to go to a class one evening a week where she can talk to people.

7.   Bill Jones studied both French and Spanish for five years at school but he failed his exams. Now he thinks he might get a better job if he has a language qualification.

8.   Sam Cartwright is out of work. He used to work in a factory as a clerk. He feels that his present skills need to be brought more up to date.

9.   Jack Tanner manages a large office. He is very busy and can only attend classes once a week. He wants to do a course which will help him to relax. He is planning to tour France and Spain on holiday.

10.   Christine Black wants to learn something practical and useful. She is not free on Wednesdays or Thursdays.

A **Advanced French Language**
Mon, Wed, 7.00 – 9.00 p.m.

This course is for people who have already done French for at least five years. It will consist of reading and discussion. There will also be lessons in French composition. There will be an examination at the end of the course, and a certificate for successful students.

B **Car Repairs**
Wed, Thurs, 7.00 – 9.00 p.m.

Save money on garage bills by learning to look after your own car and do simple repairs at home. This is a course for beginners. No previous experience is necessary.

C **First Aid**
Tuesday, 6.30 – 8.30 p.m.

Why not study for a certificate in First Aid? People on this course will learn to deal with accidents in the home and at work; what to do in the case of burns, cuts, broken bones and other common injuries.

D **Beginning Spanish**
Wednesday, 7.00 – 9.00 p.m.

Have fun learning Spanish for your holidays! It will be simple conversational Spanish – the chief purpose of the course is enjoyment. Previous knowledge of the language is unnecessary – anyone can join this course.

E **Discovering Our City's History**
Mon, Thurs, 6.30 – 9.00 p.m.

Are you curious to learn about the history which is buried beneath the streets of our city? The area has a fascinating history. This term the class will concentrate on the first five hundred years of our city's past.

F **Twentieth Century Literature**
Thursday, 7.00 – 9.00 p.m.

Study the works of the major twentieth century writers, including foreign novels and poetry in translation. This informal group will read and discuss a different novel or poem each week.

G **Keep Up Your Office Skills**
Tues, Thurs, 7.00 – 9.00 p.m.

At last an opportunity to learn to use the latest electronic office equipment. Increase your typing speed. Find out about new business methods and get to know how to run a modern office.

H **Nature Studies**
Tues, Thurs, 7.00 – 9.00 p.m.

A practical course in which students will learn to recognize plants, wild animals and birds in the countryside. There will be monthly trips to various places of interest to watch animals and birds in their natural world.

PART 3

Explanation   Part 3 contains a text of about 400 words in total, with ten sentences. The text normally comes from an advertisement, a guidebook or an information sheet. This question tests your understanding of detailed information in English. You must read the text very carefully and then check the sentences you have been given against the text. Mark **A** on your answer sheet if you think the sentences are correct and mark **B** if you think the sentences are incorrect.

Preparation   ### Exercise 1

In pairs, make as many sentences as you can about the table, using the key words in the box. These key words often appear in Part 3.

all of   the majority of   most of   some of   each of   every   both
a few of   a small number of   a large number of

Your Public Libraries

The following services are available at the public libraries in your area.

Services / Branches	High Street	Elmtree Centre	Lincoln Road	Birch Avenue	Hardwick Park	Greengarth	Thurston	Belstead
Reference section	■	■		■	■	■	■	■
Audio cassette library	■		■	■	■		■	■
Video cassette library	■			■				■
Photocopying	■	■		■			■	■
Children's library	■	■	■	■	■	■	■	■
Meeting room for hire	■				■		■	■
Local history section	■		■			■		

EXAMPLE   *Some of the branches have an audio cassette library.*

Exercise 2

You are going to look at some advertisements from people looking for penfriends.

Before you start, read the statements (1–10), then decide which of the following you must look for in the advertisements.

age(s) interests

			A	B
EXAMPLE	1.	All the people are under eighteen. ..*ages*...	☐	☐
	2	The girl from Malaysia is a sports fan.	☐	☐
	3	The youngest person can play a musical instrument.	☐	☐
	4	The person who is interested in cycling is a girl.	☐	☐
	5	The most suitable penfriend for a boy who likes outdoor sports would be Zahara.	☐	☐
	6	Karl would be a good penfriend for an eighteen year old girl who is interested in travel.	☐	☐
	7	Three of the people are willing to write to either boys or girls.	☐	☐
	8	A boy who likes winter sports would find a suitable penfriend on the list.	☐	☐
	9	All the people looking for penfriends say that they are still at school.	☐	☐
	10	One of the people wants a female penfriend who likes music.	☐	☐

Zahara, Malaysia   Box 242

I am a 16-year-old Malaysian girl and still at school. I'm interested in all kinds of outdoor sports especially tennis and hockey. At the moment I'm captain of the school hockey team. I'd like to write to a girl aged 15–17, with the same interests.

Tetsuo, Japan   Box 196

I'm a boy, aged 17. I'd like a penfriend, male or female, between 15 and 20. My interests are reading and travel. I've travelled around Europe with my friends, and I'd like to tour South America in the future. I'm also very keen on cycling.

Karen, Australia   Box 301

I'm a 15-year-old girl and I'm mad about pop music and dancing. I love going to night clubs and my favourite pop star is Michael Jackson. I also play the guitar and would like to be in a pop group myself! I'd like to write to a boy, over 16, who is interested in the same kind of things as I am.

Karl, Switzerland   Box 200

I'm still a schoolboy but I would like to be an airline pilot. I am also very keen on skiing and have competed in junior skiing competitions. I'd like to write to a boy or a girl of about my own age (16) who is interested in flying, skiing or travel.

Exercise 3

Now decide if statements 1–10 in Exercise 2 are true or false. If you agree with the statement put a tick in box **A**. If you do not agree, tick box **B**.

Test practice   **Part 3 Questions 11–20** Look at the statements below about some theatre and film events. Read the arts centre programme to decide if each statement is correct or incorrect. Mark **A** on your answer sheet if you think the statements are correct and mark **B** if you think the statements are incorrect.

Example:

Part 3		
O	A ■	B ▢

		A	**B**
11.	The Open Hand Theatre Company's *Alice* is a play.	▢	▢
12.	*Bozo's Dead* is about an event that really happened.	▢	▢
13.	The theatre shows are both suitable for young children.	▢	▢
14.	The theatre performances are more expensive than the films.	▢	▢
15.	Each of the films is longer than the performance of *Alice*.	▢	▢
16.	*Wild At Heart* is a murder thriller.	▢	▢
17.	*Dick Tracy* and *Batman* can be seen on the same day.	▢	▢
18.	One of the films was made before 1990.	▢	▢
19.	*Batman* starts at the same time as *Teenage Mutant Ninja Turtles*.	▢	▢
20.	You can buy tickets in advance for all of the films.	▢	▢

H.T.B. ARTS CENTRE   What's on in February

THEATRE

ALICE
Sat 9 February   2pm & 7.30pm
£3.75/£2.50
Open Hand Theatre Company
Running time 95 mins.
Family show – for 5 years and over.

In these New Adventures through the Looking Glass, the forest outside Old Alice's house is to be cleared, to build a theme park. In true OPEN HAND style, ALICE includes acting, dance and music. Meet old favourites and new characters, in a fast-moving new adventure for all the family.

BOZO'S DEAD
Sat 23 February   3pm
£4.50/£3
New Mime Ensemble
Running time 75 mins.

BOZO'S DEAD is about the true story of a murder in a touring circus, over 100 years ago. Pierrot (the silent clown) killed his brother and partner Auguste (the noisy clown) … But why? The crime becomes the centre of a funny and disturbing piece, which is suitable for teenagers and adults.

FILM

Tickets £2.50/£1.50
Performances at 8pm unless stated differently.

WILD AT HEART (18)   127 mins.
Wed 6 – Fri 8 February

Dir: David Lynch 1990 US
Nicholas Cage   Laura Dern   Willem Dafoe

A first class film. CAGE and his girlfriend DERN are on the run through the dangerous Deep South. They are hiding from gunmen who have been hired to kill CAGE by DERN's mother. Victims, yes – but they also have fun. It's wild at heart, strange on top. Funny, frightening and brilliant.

DICK TRACY (PG)   113 mins.
Mon 11 – Sat 16 February 6 pm
Tickets on sale 5–6pm

Dir: Warren Beatty 1990 US
Warren Beatty   Madonna

The famous detective tries to stop Big Boy and the Blank from taking over the city. A colourful and exciting film. Some parts are frightening, so think twice about taking children.

BATMAN (12)   126 mins.
Mon 11 – Sat 16 February 8.30pm
Tickets on sale 7.30 – 8.30pm
PIZZA PLUS offer 6 – 7.30pm

Dir: Tim Burton 1989 US
Michael Keaton   Jack Nicholson

A few essential questions must be asked … Is Batman a mad hero? Why does Bruce Wayne spend millions dressing up as a bat? Has NICHOLSON's Joker stolen the whole movie? Great action and excellent acting, especially by Nicholson.

TEENAGE MUTANT NINJA TURTLES (PG) 93 mins.
Mon 18 – Fri 22 February 6pm
Tickets on sale 5 – 6pm

Dir: Steve Barron 1990 US

If you've eaten Teenage Mutant Hero Turtle pizzas (marshmallow and chocolate on banana) and then cleaned your teeth with a Teenage Mutant Hero Turtle toothbrush we need say no more … If not, then get in on the craze and see for yourself. The crime fighting man-size turtles fight their enemy Shredder in an action-packed story.

PART 4

Explanation   In Part 4 you must read a text of approximately 200 words. The five questions which follow the passage test your understanding of where it comes from, the attitudes or opinions expressed in it and why it has been written. For each of the questions you must choose one of four possible answers and mark the correct letter (**A**, **B**, **C** or **D**) on your answer sheet.

Preparation   ## Exercise 1

Look at the following short passages A, B and C. You can sometimes work out what kind of writing the passage is by noticing how the writer refers to himself or herself and how the writer addresses the reader.

Passage A

I expect you would like me to tell you something about life here. Well, I think that living in Bangkok is very exciting.

I haven't lived here all my life. My family came here when I was three. But now it is my home. Nearly all my friends live here.

It's our capital city, and very big. From morning till night there are crowds of people on the main streets. Some parts of the city are very noisy. I have a long journey to school every day, but I don't mind because it is so interesting. There's always something happening in the streets. There are all kinds of people selling things – fruit, flowers, cooked food, clothes – everything you could imagine.

The area where I live is quiet, although the busiest streets are not far away. We have a garden with trees. My parents like it because it is quiet and peaceful, but I think I prefer the excitement of crowded streets and large modern buildings. I like to walk around the streets at the weekend with some other boys from my class.

Passage B

Mr Frank Gray, a businessman from the south of England, has written to the Thai government to thank them for the help he received on a recent visit to Bangkok.

Mr Gray's travel agent had booked accommodation for him at a first-class hotel in Bangkok. But on Mr Gray's arrival by air late at night, he realized that he had lost his travel papers, including his passport and traveller's cheques and the name of his hotel.

'A tour guide at the airport was extremely helpful,' said Mr Gray. 'She promised to call my travel agency in London. She also found me somewhere near the airport to stay for the night and gave me the address of the British Embassy.'

'The next morning, soon after breakfast, a taxi arrived to take me and my baggage to my hotel. I was most impressed by the way everybody looked after me,' Mr Gray added.

Passage C

Make this the year you visit Bangkok.
Your stay in Bangkok could be the most exciting experience of your life!
In Bangkok, you will see and hear things that you will never forget. You will never forget the ancient calm of fascinating golden Buddhist temples. You will never forget visiting the world's biggest and most colourful floating market, where at sunrise you can buy fresh fruit and flowers. And you will never forget the welcome you receive in beautiful restaurants where you will eat wonderful fish, straight from the sea.

Look at the pictures a, b and c. Then read sentences 1–3 (from the passages).
Decide where you would find each sentence and write a, b, or c in the box next to it.

a an advertisement

b a newspaper report

c a letter to a penfriend

1   I think that living in Bangkok is very exciting.

2   Your stay in Bangkok could be the most exciting experience of your life!

3   Mr Gray, who arrived in Bangkok by air …

Exercise 2

Think about the three different people who are writing the passages in Exercise 1. Working in pairs, look at the pictures, then decide which is the correct answer (picture a, b or c) to the questions (1–6). Put a tick in the correct box.

a the advertiser

b the reporter

c the penfriend

		a	b	c
EXAMPLE	1 Who is writing about his or her own experience?	☐	☐	☑
	2 Who is trying to persuade the reader to buy something?	☐	☐	☐
	3 Who is describing an event or events?	☐	☐	☐
	4 Who is writing to a person he or she knows?	☐	☐	☐
	5 Who is trying to attract the attention of a certain type of person?	☐	☐	☐
	6 Who is writing to give information to the general public?	☐	☐	☐

Exercise 3

Match the questions and answers.

1 What most impresses the writer of passage A about Bangkok?

2 What most impressed the writer of passage B?

3 What most impressed the writer of passage C?

4 What enjoyable experience does the writer of passage A describe?

5 What experiences does the writer of passage B describe?

6 What experiences does the writer of passage C recommend?

a *Visiting places of interest and eating special food.*

b *The many attractions for tourists visiting the city.*

c *The efficient way local people helped a visitor in difficulties.*

d *He said that it was a big modern capital city, with a lot of different things going on.*

e *Walking around the busy city streets at the weekend.*

f *A foreign visitor's problems and the way they were dealt with.*

Exercise 4

Look at the three short extracts below. Match them with the writers of the passages in Exercise 1. Write the letter of the passage (A, B or C) in the box next to each one.

1 ☐
And what's more, you can enjoy the luxury of a top class international hotel right in the centre of the city.

2 ☐
He reported that he was well taken care of all through his stay. He had nothing to complain about. 'I want to thank all the inhabitants of the city for making my trip such a success.'

3 ☐
My friends and I like to eat at some of the little stalls out in the street. They are usually quite cheap, and some of them are really good.

Test practice   **Part 4   Questions 21–25**   Read this passage and then answer the questions below. You must mark the correct letter – **A**, **B**, **C** or **D** – on your answer sheet.

Example:

Part 4
O	A B C D

Fruitibix

Do you want to be slim?
Do you worry about your family's health?

Then you should try Fruitibix, the new healthy fruit and nut biscuit. Fruitibix tastes wonderful, but it contains less sugar than most other biscuits. Each biscuit contains dried fruit and nuts, including apples, coconut and banana. Sometimes you feel like eating something between meals. Now, instead of having a chocolate bar, bite into a Fruitibix. It won't make you fat and it will keep you healthy.

At lunchtime, instead of chips or hamburgers, have a Fruitibix. It contains all the essential foods for a balanced meal. And if you are in a hurry, and you don't have time for a proper meal, Fruitibix will give you the energy to keep on going.

So whenever your children ask for something sweet, give them Fruitibix instead of cakes or chocolate. They will love the taste and it won't harm their teeth.

Discover **Fruitibix**. It's on your supermarket shelves now!

21. This is from

    A   a letter.

    B   a magazine article.

    C   a student's notebook.

    D   an advertisement.

22. The writer wants to

    A   persuade people to buy a product.

    B   explain why people use this product.

    C   give advice about healthy living.

    D   compare this with other sorts of food.

23. Why, in the writer's opinion, should people eat Fruitibix instead of chocolate?

    A   Fruitibix tastes better than chocolate.

    B   Fruitibix contains more fat than chocolate.

    C   Fruitibix is cheaper and easier to eat than chocolate.

    D   Fruitibix is healthier and less fattening than chocolate.

24. Why does the writer say that Fruitibix is useful when you are in a hurry?

    A   You don't need to cook it.

    B   You can buy Fruitibix everywhere.

    C   It is as good as a proper meal.

    D   It won't be harmful to your teeth.

25. Which of these people ought to buy Fruitibix?

    A   Mrs Brown is looking for something special to serve for dessert at a dinner party she is giving for her boss and his wife.

    B   Mr Green wants something to take with him to the office. He is going to be very busy tomorrow, and he thinks he might not have time for lunch.

    C   Mr Taylor is going on a fishing trip and he wants to take something to eat with him. Some kinds of fruit, like bananas, make him feel sick, but he enjoys salty food.

    D   Mrs Booth's baby daughter was ill yesterday. She is getting better now, but the doctor has advised Mrs Booth to give her liquid food without any sugar or salt in it.

PART 5

Explanation For Part 5 you have to read a short passage of about 100–150 words. It could be from a newspaper article, a letter or a book. This question tests your knowledge of vocabulary and grammatical structure. The passage has ten missing words and these spaces are numbered 26–35. For each space a set of four words is given below the passage. For numbers 26–35 you must choose the best word to complete the passage. When you have done this mark the correct letter – **A, B, C** or **D** – on your answer sheet.

Example:

Preparation ### Exercise 1

Here is a passage with eighteen words missing, but you can understand a lot of it, even without the missing words. Read the passage and answer the questions about it.

The Meadow Park Zoo, which ^{1}...... three months ago, is already ^{2}...... large numbers of visitors. The zoo has ^{3}...... especially popular with families.

'My children were delighted when they ^{4}...... here last month,' said one mother. 'So they ^{5}...... me to bring them back today.'

The new zoo is quite small, compared with other similar ^{6}...... You won't find any large and dangerous animals such as ^{7}...... or tigers in cages. Instead, there is a children's zoo, where children can handle little animals like rabbits and ^{8}...... They can also have rides on a camel, a ^{9}...... or an elephant. The zoo has a working farm, too, with cows, sheep, ^{10}......, ducks and chickens.

'Lots of children ^{11}...... cities don't understand what happens ^{12}...... a farm. It's important ^{13}...... them to see for themselves where their milk and eggs come ^{14}......,' a member of the zoo's staff explained.

Most visitors spend at least four hours there, so ^{15}...... expect to have some kind of meal at the zoo. ^{16}...... has got a large restaurant ^{17}...... serves snacks, as well as a pleasant and convenient picnic area, where visitors can eat ^{18}...... own food.

1 Has the zoo been open a long time?
2 What kind of people does the zoo attract?
3 What special attractions does the zoo provide for children?
4 What can children find out on the farm?
5 Why does the zoo need to provide somewhere for its visitors to eat?

Exercise 2

When you have decided what the passage is about, you have to choose the right words to fill the spaces. The words you choose must:

1 fit into the space grammatically.
2 have the right meaning.

EXAMPLE 1   *Nowadays farmers .... cows by machine.*

Which of these nonsense words would fit into the space grammatically?

zonked   zonking   zonks   zonk

The grammar tells you that:
- you need a verb in this sentence
- the verb should be in the present tense (*Nowadays ...*)
- the subject of the verb is plural (*farmers ...*).

So *zonk* is the only word that fits grammatically.

Now choose a word for the same space, but this time, think about the meaning. (All four choices will fit grammatically.)

EXAMPLE 2   *Milk production used to need a lot of workers. Nowadays farmers .... cows by machine. This means that fewer workers are required.*

teach   milk   see   arrange

You know that the answer is going to be something that farmers do to cows, and that it is something that can be done by machine. The first sentence in the paragraph is about milk production. Therefore, you know that *milk* is the correct answer. (Note that *milk* can be a verb as well as a noun.)

Now read the passage in Exercise 1 again and look at the choices below. Circle the correct answer, A, B, C or D.

- **Forms of the verb**   For 1–5 decide which is the correct form of the verb to use in the sentence.

EXAMPLE   1   **A** open   **B** opens   **C** opening   **(D)** opened

       2   **A** attract   **B** attracts   **C** attracting   **D** attracted

       3   **A** prove   **B** proves   **C** proving   **D** proved

       4   **A** come   **B** comes   **C** coming   **D** came

       5   **A** persuade   **B** persuades   **C** persuading   **D** persuaded

- **Meaning**   For 6–10 decide which word makes sense in the context.

       6   **A** attractions   **B** events   **C** parties   **D** schools

       7   **A** rats   **B** birds   **C** lions   **D** fish

       8   **A** crocodiles   **B** mice   **C** hippos   **D** bears

       9   **A** pig   **B** snake   **C** tiger   **D** horse

    10   **A** monkeys   **B** hippos   **C** tigers   **D** goats

- **Prepositions**   For 11–14 decide which is the correct preposition for the space.

   11   **A** over   **B** about   **C** from   **D** with

   12   **A** up   **B** for   **C** across   **D** on

   13   **A** for   **B** up   **C** at   **D** of

   14   **A** after   **B** from   **C** off   **D** away

- **Pronouns**   For 15–18 decide which is the right pronoun for the sentence.

   15   **A** they   **B** it   **C** them   **D** our

   16   **A** You   **B** It   **C** He   **D** They

   17   **A** who   **B** they   **C** it   **D** which

   18   **A** its   **B** they   **C** their   **D** our

Exercise 3

Read passages A and B and look at the pictures. Say which picture shows what is described in the passages.

Passage A

SOUTHFIELD FILM CLUB

There will be a committee meeting [1].......... Saturday evening at 7.30. We are going to [2].......... the plans for the party [3].......... December.

The [4].......... will be held in the school hall. There will be tea and coffee in the dining room [5].......... the meeting.

I hope all committee members will try to attend [6].......... this meeting is very important.

Catherine Fry
Club Secretary

Passage B

I went to the film club committee meeting [1].......... Saturday. The meeting was [2].......... 7.30 in the evening. There was a [3].......... about the plans for the party on 15th December.

We [4].......... in the school hall. [5].......... we went into the dining room where we had tea and coffee.

It was a very important meeting [6].......... all the committee members were there.

1

2

3

Exercise 4

Find the answers to these questions about passages A and B in Exercise 3.
1 Which passage, A or B, refers to something that happened in the past?
2 Which passage, A or B, refers to something that will happen in the future?
3 Which passage, A or B, describes a personal experience?

Exercise 5

These are the missing words from passages A and B in Exercise 3. Put them in the correct spaces.

after   afterwards   because   discuss   discussion   in   last   meeting   met
next   at   so

Test practice   **Part 5 Questions 26–35**   Read the passage below and choose the word that best fits each space. Mark the correct letter – **A**, **B**, **C** or **D** – on your answer sheet.

Example:

How are things with you? Since I saw you last, I've been very ill. By the time I arrived home after seeing you on Monday, I ²⁶.............. an awful headache.

I thought that perhaps my eyes were tired ²⁷.............. I'd been working so hard, so I took some aspirins and went to bed. However, when I woke up the next morning the headache was ²⁸.............. than ever, and my throat was sore. I tried to get up but my arms and legs ²⁹.............. stiff.

I saw the doctor and she ³⁰.............. me I had a temperature. She said I probably had flu. She advised me to take some medicine and ³¹.............. in bed. The medicine tasted horrible and it didn't make ³².............. feel any better. I felt sick and I didn't want to eat anything at all, although I was very ³³..............

I have almost ³⁴.............. now, and I'm going to start work again tomorrow. I still have a slight cold and a cough, but my chest doesn't hurt when I ³⁵..............

Can we meet on Saturday? I'm looking forward to seeing you.

26.   A felt   B had   C was   D caught

27.   A as   B though   C while   D during

28.   A worse   B hard   C more   D painful

29.   A sensed   B moved   C felt   D looked

30.   A examined   B told   C denied   D said

31.   A stay   B stayed   C staying   D stays

32.   A some   B me   C them   D its

33.   A ill   B heavy   C hungry   D thirsty

34.   A improved   B decided   C recovered D succeeded

35.   A breathe   B ache   C cure   D bleed

Reading test

Part 1 Questions 1–5 Look at the five pictures of signs below. Someone asks you what each sign means. For each sign mark the correct letter – **A**, **B**, **C** or **D** – on your answer sheet.

Example:

Part 1
O | A B C D

1.

PLEASE KEEP ENTRANCE FREE
NO BICYCLES
AGAINST THIS FENCE

   A You can take your bicycle in through this entrance free of charge.

   B You must not leave your bicycle by the fence because it will be in the way of the entrance.

   C Bicycle riders are not allowed to enter because they might lean against the fence.

   D There is a fence inside, so you must leave your bicycle outside the entrance.

2.

GUESTS ARE REQUESTED TO HAND IN ALL KEYS AT THE DESK WHEN THEY CHECK OUT

   A When you leave the hotel give in your keys at the desk.

   B Pick up your keys at the desk when you arrive.

   C Check at the desk that you have the right keys.

   D If you lose your keys, pay for them at the desk.

3.

TOILET OUT OF ORDER
PLEASE USE STAFF TOILET UPSTAIRS

   A Staff are not allowed to use this toilet. They must go upstairs.

   B This toilet has been closed. A new toilet has been opened upstairs.

   C Staff are mending the toilets at the moment, including the ones upstairs.

   D This toilet is broken, but you can use the ones upstairs.

4.

10% OFF ALL ELECTRICAL GOODS
SPECIAL OFFER FOR CHRISTMAS SEASON ONLY

   A Ten per cent of the electrical goods have been sold for Christmas.

   B Nine out of ten electrical things make good Christmas presents.

   C For Christmas, all the electrical goods cost ten per cent less.

   D Electrical goods will be cheaper after Christmas.

5.

A It is dangerous to queue on the other side.

B Stand in a line if you want to cross to the other side.

C It is safer to wait in a queue on the other side.

D Queue on the other side for information about safety.

Part 2 Questions 6–10 The following people are choosing books to read. Look at the information about new books. Decide which book each person should get. Mark the correct letter – **A** to **H** – on the answer sheet.

Example:

Part 2								
O	A	B	C	D	E	F	G	H
	■	□	□	□	□	□	□	□

 The Wild Wood
by Rex Dobson

A band of robbers break into a house and kidnap a rich girl. Fortunately, there is one man who can find their secret hiding place and rescue her. The cruel leader of the band wants to murder the girl. There is a scream . . . then . . .

 Vote for Hannah Harvey
by E. L. Thornaway

Hannah Harvey, a close relation of the Prime Minister, wins an election. Hannah is hard-working and plans to become a great woman politician. Then she agrees to help a friend who is in trouble and suddenly things start to go wrong . . .

 Singing on the Shore
by Margery Pleasant

Another romantic novel from Margery Pleasant. The heroine, Maria, is a poor girl who goes to the seaside to work as a waitress. She falls in love with a famous singer, but he is engaged to a beautiful blonde dancer. Maria is desperately unhappy.

G **Steam and Smoke**
by Mark O'Brien

This novel is set in the 19th century, in the early days of railway transport. It tells of the battle between two men; a young engineer, Joshua Dobson and his enemy, the rich landowner, Jasper March.

 Behind the Wheel
by Bert Dixon

Bert Dixon started to keep a diary as soon as he got his driving licence. Now a well-known professional racing driver, he tells a story full of race tracks, sharp bends, cars on fire, burst tyres and more than a few crashes.

 A Man at War
by Henry Martin

The true story of a soldier who joined the army at nineteen. Henry Martin tells of battles, of helicopters exploding, of bombs dropping, of bullets flying. Taken prisoner by the enemy, he manages to escape from prison by night and get away over the mountains.

 Elephant Morning
by Esther Motsumi

The author was the first woman from her village to qualify as a doctor. This is the true story of her life running a clinic in southern Africa. She writes beautifully about the people she met and their relationship with the animals in Africa.

 Home Decoration
by Alice and Peter Saunders

This book gives step-by-step instructions for painting and decorating all kinds of houses. It is full of useful ideas, with lots of pictures in colour.

6. Joanna Brown does not like novels. She prefers reading about people's real-life experiences. She is interested in reading about far-away places and animals.

7. Eric Macadam likes adventure stories, but he does not like stories about the past. He read one of E.L. Thornaway's books last year, but thought it was rather boring. He hates love stories.

8. Caroline Martin likes stories about women, although she does not care for love stories. She prefers to read about strong successful women, whose lives are rather like her own. She is a businesswoman who lives in London.

9. Jonathan Cuthbert is nineteen. He is interested in transport, and although he likes excitement, he does not like war stories. In fact, he prefers non-fiction to fiction.

10. Gerald Donaldson is a politician, but he wants to relax on his holiday by reading something completely different from his own life. He thinks he would like to try a love story. A novel set in the world of entertainment would be ideal.

Part 3 Questions 11–20 Look at the statements below about passengers arriving at an airport. Read the text to decide if each statement is correct or incorrect. Mark **A** on your answer sheet if you think the notes are correct and mark **B** if you think the notes are incorrect.

Example:

IMPORTANT INFORMATION FOR PASSENGERS

Arrival
When the plane lands, you are requested to keep your seat belt fastened until the light goes off and remain in your seat until the plane stops moving. This is for your own comfort and safety.

Leaving the airport
If you are ending your journey at this airport, you should go up the escalator to passport control and customs. If you are travelling further by rail or coach, you will find an information desk outside the customs hall, as well as a bank where you can change money.

Catching another flight
If you are planning to change planes, you should follow the signs to the waiting lounge, where you should check in and wait to board your connecting flight. There will be an announcement when your flight is due to take off. Our ground staff will be happy to help you.

Leaving the plane
All passengers leaving the plane should make sure that they take everything with them. If you have checked in any luggage, you should remember to collect it from the baggage area inside the airport.

Continuing on this flight
We regret that passengers who are continuing their journey on this flight may not get off the plane. You may not smoke while the plane is on the ground.

Thank you for flying with us. We hope to be able to welcome you on board again soon.

11. All passengers must leave the aeroplane.

12. You must wait until the light goes out before undoing your seat belt.

13. Passengers who are leaving the airport must first go to passport control.

14. Passengers continuing by another plane must go through customs.

15. You can change money before you go to passport control.

16. You must go up the escalator to the waiting lounge if you are changing planes.

17. Passengers in the waiting lounge will hear an announcement when their plane is ready to leave.

18. No one is allowed to smoke in the airport.

19. The aeroplane is going on to another place after some of the passengers get off.

20. Passengers who are leaving the plane should check that they have not left anything behind.

Part 4 Questions 21–25 Read this passage and then answer the questions below. Mark the correct letter – **A**, **B**, **C** or **D** – on your answer sheet.

Example:

The Face in the Mirror

The play now on at the New Theatre as part of the Easter Arts Festival is not among the best plays for which the director, Amy Fielding, has been responsible.

The action takes place in the home of Professor Spear. One night his landlady comes to the house for a chat. After inviting her in, the professor hears a sound and, thinking it is a burglar come to rob the house, fires his gun. By mistake, the wrong person is shot and the thief gets away.

The scene of the second act is a law court, in which everyone waits to find out if the professor is guilty of murder.

I did not care for the acting in some cases. Norman Jones is normally seen in comedy and is not satisfactory as the professor. He does not look like a wise old man. Also, Simon Fry, as the servant, shouted at the top of his voice all through the play. The hit of the evening, however, was James Smith as the judge.

On the whole, the play appeared to me to be a little out of date. I can think of many other plays which would have been more suitable for a group of clever young actors to perform.

The play continues until the end of the month.

21. This passage is from

    A   a review of a play.

    B   an introduction to a book.

    C   a letter.

    D   an advertisement.

22. What is the writer trying to do?

    A   Give advice to the writer of the play.

    B   Warn people not to go and see the play.

    C   Give his own opinion of the play.

    D   Persuade the director to change the play.

23. The writer's opinion about the play was that

   A   there were not enough actors for the parts.

   B   the actors would have performed better in a modern play.

   C   the play was being performed at the wrong time of the year.

   D   the play was a comedy, but the audience did not find it amusing.

24. The writer thought the actor who played the professor was unsatisfactory because

   A   he made the audience laugh too much.

   B   he did not look like a professor.

   C   he had the wrong kind of moustache.

   D   he was not clever enough to play the part.

25. Who will probably enjoy the play?

I don't care much for serious subjects. I like comedies, especially about the young. Norman Jones is great, so young and lively. I like the way he jumps about the stage. He never stands still.

A

I only like going to the theatre when there's something on with a lot of songs. Simon Fry is a good singer; I saw him in a show last year. I hope he'll be singing again when I next go to the theatre.

B

I really prefer plays with a good story. I like to wonder about what is going to happen in the end. I like fights, but I like to see the guilty person punished in the end. I'm a great fan of James Smith.

C

I prefer modern plays. This director did one that I liked last year. There were a group of actors on a bare stage without any scenery. It showed what was wrong with modern society.

D

Part 5 Questions 26–35 Read the article below and choose the word that best fits each space. Mark the correct letter – **A**, **B**, **C** or **D** – on your answer sheet.

Example:

In the match between Parkfield School and Greenport Football Club which took place at Greenport ^{26}.......... Saturday the Parkfield team beat Greenport by three goals to two.

The last time the two ^{27}.......... met Greenport won by three goals to nil, so Parkfield were making a great ^{28}.......... to win this game.

In the first half of the game, Greenport ^{29}.......... leading by two goals, and Parkfield's position looked hopeless. However, Greenport made a number of ^{30}.......... mistakes during the second half. This was after their star player, Brown, missed the ball, slipped and ^{31}.......... heavily, injuring his left ankle.

Parkfield then scored two lucky ^{32}.........., and in the few minutes before the finish, Prescott shot the ball ^{33}.......... the net for them, bringing the score to three goals to two.

Parkfield have ^{34}.......... well this season, and their fans have good reason to be proud. Greenport too, have had good results up to now. Out of the last five games played, this is the first game they have ^{35}..........

26. A next   B every   C once   D last

27. A dates   B teams   C fights   D events

28. A effort   B chance   C journey   D competition

29. A had   B were   C seemed   D made

30. A careless   B many   C generous   D deep

31. A kicked   B bent   C fell   D ran

32. A goals   B players   C matches   D teams

33. A up   B through   C into   D beneath

34. A been   B lost   C made   D played

35. A won   B beaten   C missed   D lost

Writing

PART 1

Explanation   In Part 1 you are asked to read five sentences and to rewrite them. The beginning of each new sentence is written for you. You must complete the new sentence so that it has the same meaning as the first sentence. All five sentences are about the same subject. You can use the exam paper for your rough answers, but you must write your final answer on your answer sheet.

EXAMPLE   It is possible to obtain change for phone calls at the counter.
You can *obtain change for phone calls at the counter.*

Preparation   ### Exercise 1

There are a lot of ways of saying the same thing. Working in pairs, find sentences in this advertisement which have the same meaning as sentences 1–10.

SUN AND SEA HOLIDAY FLATS

This block of flats was built five years ago. It has four floors, with four large flats on each floor. All the flats on the upper floors can be reached by lift.

Each flat has a living room, two bedrooms, kitchen and bathroom. There is also a small store room which can be used as an extra bedroom.

All the flats have air-conditioning. Some have central heating during the winter months. Tenants have a choice between gas and electric cookers in the kitchens. New up-to-date showers were installed in all the bathrooms last year. Flats can be rented weekly, fortnightly or monthly. It is not possible to rent a flat for less than a week. The rent for flats with a sea view is higher.

There is a manager in attendance. The manager's office is in the entrance hall on the ground floor of the building.

EXAMPLE   1   Tenants can choose between gas and electric cookers in the kitchens.
Tenants have a choice between gas and electric cookers in the kitchens.

2   You can also use the small store room as an extra bedroom.

3   They built the flats five years ago.

4   During the winter months, there is central heating in some of the flats.

5   There are four floors, with four large flats on each floor in the block.

6   Last year the owners installed new up-to-date showers in all the bathrooms.

7   You cannot rent a flat for less than a week.

8   The manager has an office in the entrance hall on the ground floor.

9   The flats which do not have a sea view are cheaper to rent.

10   If you take the lift, you can reach all the flats on the upper floors.

Exercise 2

In the test some sentences may have to be changed from passive to active or from active to passive. Read this letter.

SUN AND SEA HOLIDAY FLATS

Dear Mr and Mrs Green,

We are happy to confirm your booking for Flat Number 6 for the fortnight starting 6th July. Here is some further information about the flats:

1 All necessary kitchen utensils, including kettle, pans, knives, forks, spoons, cups, saucers, plates, bowls, etc. are supplied by the management.
2 All carpets, curtains, etc. are cleaned every season.
3 The manager of the flats collects rubbish daily from all the flats. Dustbins can be found beside the back door.
4 Laundry can be done in the basement, where there are washing machines. The manager can arrange dry-cleaning.
5 The manager can order milk and groceries for you. These will be delivered to your flat.
6 All doors and windows can be locked.
7 Cars must not be left in front of the building. Owners must park their cars in the parking space behind the flats.
8 All breakages and damage to the flats must be paid for. The manager will inspect the flat at the end of your stay.
9 The full rent for your holiday must be paid one month in advance.

We hope that you will enjoy your stay in the Sun and Sea Flats. Please write to us if you have any queries.

Yours sincerely,

Amy Roberts

Letting Agent

Look at these examples of active and passive sentences:

active *The Greens **have rented** flat number 6 for two weeks in July.*
passive *Flat number 6 **has been rented** for two weeks in July [by the Greens].*

In the passive sentence, the 'agent' of the verb is *the Greens*. If there is no agent in a passive sentence, you can substitute *you, one*, etc. when you change it into an active sentence.

EXAMPLE   **passive** *All the windows can be locked.*

active $\left\{\begin{array}{l} You \, ... \\ One \, ... \\ Tenants \, ... \end{array}\right\}$ *can lock all the windows.*

When you change an active sentence into a passive one, you can often miss out the agent.

EXAMPLE   **active** *You can use the spare bedroom as a store room.*
passive *The spare bedroom can be used as a store room.*

Working in pairs, make sentences, active and passive, about the holiday flats. Use the words given below (1–10). The first one has been done for you, as an example.

EXAMPLE   1   damage
Damage to the flats must be paid for.
You must pay for damage to the flats.
or *Tenants must pay for damage to the flats.*

2   cups and saucers   7   rubbish
3   laundry   8   dry-cleaning
4   cars   9   dustbins
5   rent   10   groceries
6   curtains

Exercise 3 🔈

Listen to this conversation between Mrs Taylor and the booking clerk of the holiday company. Listen for any examples of sentences using *there is/there are* or *has/have*.

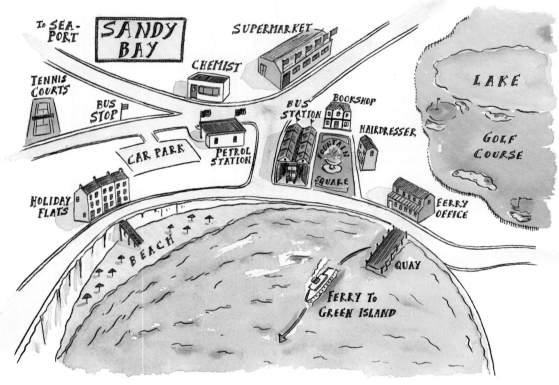

Sentences with *there is/there are* can be changed to sentences with *has/have*.

EXAMPLE   1   *There is a golf course in Sandy Bay.*
Sandy Bay has a golf course.

2   *There is a lovely beach at the bottom of the cliffs in Sandy Bay.*
Sandy Bay has a lovely beach at the bottom of the cliffs.

Look at the map of Sandy Bay, then look at the other things on Mrs Taylor's list on the next page. Make sentences like the ones in the examples, using *there is/there are* and *has/have*.

(In some of your answers you can use prepositions, for example, *in, near, opposite, close to* to say where the things are, but it is not possible in all the answers.)

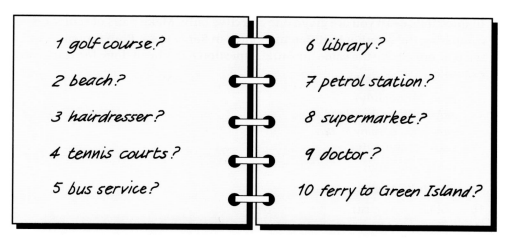

1 golf course?

2 beach?

3 hairdresser?

4 tennis courts?

5 bus service?

6 library?

7 petrol station?

8 supermarket?

9 doctor?

10 ferry to Green Island?

Exercise 4

Look at the information about these two hotels and the climate in Santa Rosa.

HOTELS IN SANTA ROSA

Seven Stars Hotel

Rooms: 48
Distance from ● Airport: 25km
● Santa Rosa: 4km

Blue Moon Hotel

Rooms: 210
Distance from ● Airport: 17km
● Santa Rosa: 2km

Climate: Santa Rosa	June	July	August
average temperature	22°C	25°C	28°C
hours of sunshine per day	8	7	8
rainy days	3	5	2

Use these adjectives to make pairs of sentences comparing the two hotels. Both sentences in the pair must have the same meaning. The first pair has been done for you as an example.

EXAMPLE
1 big/small
The Blue Moon Hotel is bigger than the Seven Stars Hotel.
The Seven Stars Hotel is smaller than the Blue Moon Hotel.

2 near/far (the airport)

3 old/new

4 many/few (rooms)

5 near/far (Santa Rosa)

In questions 6–10 you are given one adjective only. Make pairs of sentences comparing the weather in different months in Santa Rosa. Both sentences in the pair must have the same meaning. Question 6 has been done for you as an example.

EXAMPLE
6 rainy (June/July)
July is rainier than June.
June is not as rainy as July.

7 warm (June/July)

8 wet (June/July)

9 dry (July/August)

10 hot (July/August)

Exercise 5

Look at the two sentences in the example. They have the same meaning, but one uses *by ...-ing* and the other uses *if*.

EXAMPLE
You can get to the airport by phoning for a taxi.
If you want to get to the airport, you should phone for a taxi.

Look at the map and then answer the questions using both kinds of sentence.

1 How can you get onto the beach from the hotel?

2 Is it possible to spend the evening dancing?

3 How can you hire a boat?

4 Can we get a cold drink on the beach?

5 How do you get to town if you haven't got a car?

6 Where can we have a swim?

7 How can we hire a car?

8 What's the best way to get a good suntan?

9 We've been told you can catch fish around here. Can we hire a boat?

10 How can you get to Palm Island?

Exercise 6

Sometimes you can change sentences by changing a verb to a noun or a noun to a verb.

EXAMPLE *There is **a choice** for buyers between two bedrooms and three bedrooms.* (noun)
*Buyers can **choose** between two bedrooms and three bedrooms.* (verb)

Complete this table of verbs and nouns.

Verb	Noun	Verb	Noun	Verb	Noun
choose	choice	advise	advice	move	
correct		announce		weigh	
	success	improve		pronounce	
attract			practice	direct	
	meaning	develop		inform	
describe			invasion	depart	
invite		meet		educate	

Exercise 7

Now change these sentences by using a verb or a noun. The first one has been done for you.

EXAMPLE 1 He gave a description of his new house in a letter.
His letter *described his new house.*

2 The flats were advertised in the local newspaper.
There was ...

3 They received some advice from their neighbours.
Their neighbours ...

4 The weight of the package is 2.5 kilograms.
The package ...

5 There was an announcement about the winners.
Somebody ...

6 They discussed the problem for three hours.
Their ...

7 He received part of his education in France.
He was ...

8 There's going to be a new development.
Something new is ...

Test practice

Part 1 Questions 1–5 Here are some sentences about visiting an art gallery. For each question, finish the second sentence so that it means the same as the first. The second sentence is started for you. Write only the missing words on your answer sheet. You may use this page for any rough work.

Example: I paid £3 for my entrance ticket.

My entrance ticket *cost £3.* ....

1. Catalogues are available at the desk.

   You can ....

2. These paintings were done in France in 1926.

   The artist ....

3. The last exhibition of the artist's work was held by the Fine Arts Society in 1966.

   The Fine Arts Society ....

4. Private collectors lent some of the paintings in the exhibition.

   Some of ....

5. All umbrellas must be left at the desk.

   You ....

PART 2

Explanation In Part 2 you are asked to complete a form which you must fill in with personal details such as your name and address. There are ten items in all, and each should be answered with a word, a number or a short phrase. You can use the exam paper for your rough answers but you must write your final answer on the answer sheet.

Preparation ### Exercise 1

Look at the form on page 46 which was completed by a visitor to this hobbies exhibition.
What can you find out about Joe from the form? Answer *True, False* or *I don't know*. The first one has been done for you.

EXAMPLE   1   Joe visited the exhibition on the first day it was open. *False*

2   Joe read about the exhibition in the local newspaper.

3   Joe liked everything about the exhibition.

4   Joe is British.

5   Joe is a teenager.

6   Joe was interested in the cycling stand.

7   Joe came by bus to the exhibition.

8   Joe's initials are J.S.D.

9   Joe doesn't have a job yet.

10   Joe spent all day at the exhibition.

Basketball
Boats
Cameras
Camping
Coins
Cycling
Dance
Football   Motorbikes
Guitars   Music
Hi–fi   Painting
Hockey   Photography
Jazz   Sailing
Jogging   Ski–ing
Models   Stamps
              Swimming
              Table–tennis
              Tennis
              Video
              Walking
              Wind–surfing

Sports and Hobbies
31 October – 12 April

19th Annual
Exhibition

19th Sports and Hobbies Exhibition

VISITOR SURVEY

Date: ..6 November..............

Personal details

Surname: .....Smedley...... First name(s): ...Joe David.........

Nationality: ..British........ Occupation: ......Student.........

Age: (tick your age group)

under 12 ☐   12 – 16 ✓   17 – 25 ☐

26 – 39 ☐   40 – 59 ☐   over 60 ☐

1   How did you hear about the exhibition?
....On the local radio...

2   What are your hobbies?
....Swimming and stamp collecting.................................

3   Which stand did you find most interesting?
.....The windsurfing stand..

4   What else did you like about the exhibition?
......The atmosphere was very friendly............................

5   Was there anything that you did not like?
......The coffee shop was too expensive...........................

Exercise 2

Read this information about Françoise, then fill in her form.

Seventeen-year-old Françoise Dupont comes from Paris. She is an office worker. She visited the hobbies exhibition on the day after Joe. She read about the exhibition in the newspaper. She was keen to go to the exhibition because she is interested in photography and collecting coins. She found the photography stand very interesting and spent a lot of time there. She was also impressed by the video display. She found the whole exhibition very lively and colourful, but she had a lot of difficulty finding the coin stand, because the plan of the exhibition in the programme was rather confusing.

19th Sports and Hobbies Exhibition

VISITOR SURVEY

Date: *7 November*

Personal details

Surname: *Dupont*   First name(s): ....

Nationality: ....   Occupation: ....

Age: (tick your age group)

under 12 ☐   12 – 16 ☐   17 – 25 ☐

26 – 39 ☐   40 – 59 ☐   over 60 ☐

1   How did you hear about the exhibition?
   ....

2   What are your hobbies?
   ....

3   Which stand did you find most interesting?
   ....

4   What else did you like about the exhibition?
   ....

5   Was there anything that you did not like?
   ....

Exercise 3

Look at the picture of a student's room and answer the questions with your partner.

1 What is the student's name?
2 What furniture is there in the room?
3 Are there any electrical appliances in the room?
4 Is the room in good condition?
5 Is there enough room to store things?

Exercise 4

Use your answers to fill in the form.

STUDENT ACCOMMODATION SURVEY

Name ....   Room No ....

Please list the furniture in the room. ....
....

Please list the electrical appliances in the room. ....
....

Are there any repairs that need to be done? ....
....

Where do you keep your food? ....

List any extra furniture you need. ....
....

Signature ....

Test practice   **Part 2 Questions 6–15** You are going to apply for a holiday job through a students' employment organization. Fill in the form below, giving details about yourself. You can use this page for your rough answers but you must write your final answer on your answer sheet.

STUDENT JOB CENTRE

Application for holiday work

Please supply the following information:

Surname (6) .... Initials .... [*Mr/Mrs/Miss/Ms]

* Please cross out as appropriate

Address (7) ....

....

Date of birth (day, month, year) (8) ....

PLEASE give a telephone number so that we can contact you if a job is available.

(9) ....

Type of job you want to do (10) ....

Number of weeks you can work (11) ....

Preferred hours of work (12) ....

Do you have any special skills? (13) ....

....

What jobs have you done before? (14) ....

....

Signature (15)..

PART 3

Explanation Part 3 gives you the chance to write more freely in English, in an informal letter. You may be asked to write about a recent experience, about your plans for the future, or about your opinion on a particular subject. You will be given some ideas about what sort of things to write and sometimes there are pictures to help you. You should write about 100 words. You can use the exam paper for your rough answer, but you have to write your final answer on the back of your answer sheet.

Preparation ### Exercise 1

Look at this programme for a weekend conference for students who are planning to study in Britain for a short time.

WEEKEND CONFERENCE

Living in Britain

Saturday		**Sunday**	
10.00 a.m.	Talk: Family Life in Britain	9.00 a.m.	Talk: Transport in Britain
11.00 a.m.	Video: London Sightseeing	11.00 a.m.	Visiting the Doctor – What to do if you are ill

* * * LUNCH * * *

2.00 p.m.	Talk: The History of Britain	2.00 p.m.	Talk: Where to Study
		3.00 p.m.	Your Questions Answered – Discussion with students who have returned from Britain

* * * TEA * * *

8.00 p.m.	Saturday Night Disco	6.00 p.m.	Conference ends

Imagine that you took part in the conference. Decide how useful or interesting you would have found the different activities at the conference. Complete the following table, giving each activity a mark from 1 to 5 on this basis:

1 = not at all   2 = not very   3 = quite   4 = very   5 = extremely

For example, if you would have found the talk on 'The History of Britain' *quite interesting* but *not very useful* then write *3* and *2* in the correct boxes.

	Useful	Interesting
1 Family Life in Britain		
2 London Sightseeing		
3 History of Britain		
4 Disco		
5 Transport in Britain		
6 Visiting the Doctor		
7 Where to Study		
8 Your Questions Answered		

Exercise 2

Imagine that you are going to write a letter about the conference to a friend.
You could plan your letter in two different ways. Look at the two plans below.

Working in pairs, decide in which plan (A or B) and in which section (2A, 3B etc.) you would find these sentences. Write the number of the section in the box next to the sentence. The first one has been done for you.

EXAMPLE

1 I thought that the best part of the conference was ... ⟨2B⟩

2 There were two talks on Sunday morning ... ☐

3 There were some other activities during the conference ... ☐

4 I must tell you about a conference I attended last weekend ... ☐

5 I'm afraid I did not like the ... about ... ☐

6 When the conference was over, I felt tired, but ... ☐

7 After lunch on Saturday, we ... ☐

Exercise 3

This letter was written following Plan A (in Exercise 2). Complete the table of time expressions which appear in the letter. The answers for the first two paragraphs have been done for you.

Dear ...,

Thank you for your letter. I enjoyed hearing about your trip. You asked me what I have been doing. I must tell you about a conference I attended last weekend. It was for students who were planning to study in Britain.

The conference started on Saturday morning, when there was a talk on family life followed by a video about sightseeing in London. I liked the talk, which was fairly interesting, but I thought the video was boring.

Then on Saturday afternoon there was a talk about history. The speaker was very good but I thought the talk lasted too long. The next thing on the programme was a great disco in the evening.

There were two talks on Sunday morning. The first one was a very useful talk about transport. I took a lot of notes. The second talk, which I found rather confusing, was about visiting the doctor in Britain.

After lunch on Sunday we heard first about the best places to study in Britain. This was quite useful, I decided. However, the last thing on the programme was my favourite. It was a discussion with some students who went to study in Britain last year. We all asked a lot of questions, and they told us about their experiences.

When the conference was over, I felt tired but I had learnt a lot and made some new friends. I now feel much more confident about going abroad to study.

Paragraph	Time expressions
Opening paragraph	... *last weekend*
2A	... *on Saturday morning, when...* ... *followed by...*
3A	
4A	
5A	
Closing paragraph	

Exercise 4

Look at the table below. Working in pairs, fill in the first column (+ , − or o) by deciding if each adjective is positive (+), negative (−) or neutral (o). Then tick the boxes to show which adjectives you could use to describe the things above (*a person, a place, etc.*). The first two have been done for you as examples.

	+, − or o	a person	a place	entertainment	a sporting activity	a book	a lecture or talk	the weather
amusing	+	✓		✓		✓	✓	
disgusting	−	✓	✓	✓		✓	✓	✓
cheerful								
embarrassing								
good-looking								
kind								
lovely								
miserable								
perfect								
strange								
typical								

Look at these expressions you can use when you want to give your opinion about something.

I think   In my opinion   I believe   I feel [that]   It seems to me that
I am quite certain that   Personally, I feel that

Working in pairs, discuss these questions using the adjectives and expressions from this exercise (and any others you can think of).

1 What do you think of people who work in hospitals?
2 What's your opinion of horror films?
3 What do you think of football matches on TV?
4 What's your opinion of people who read comics?
5 What do you think of your city centre?
6 What kind of weather do you like/dislike?

Exercise 5

Look at the letter about the conference in Exercise 3. It was written using Plan A (from Exercise 2). Rewrite the letter using Plan B. (Remember that you do not need to change the opening and closing paragraphs.) Write about 100 words.

Test practice **Part 3** You have had a special meal at this restaurant with a group of friends. Write about it in a letter to an English-speaking friend. Write about 100 words. The address is not necessary. You can use this page for your rough answer but you must write your final answer on your answer sheet.

Dear
I hope you are well. ....
....
....
....
....
....
....
....
....
....
....

Writing test

Part 1 Questions 1–5 Here are some sentences about the Post Office. For each question, finish the second sentence so that it means the same as the first. The second sentence is started for you. Write only the missing words on your answer sheet. You may use this page for any rough work.

Example: It is possible to obtain change for phone calls at the counter.

You can *obtain change for phone calls at the counter.* ....

1. There is a complete set of telephone directories in the Post Office.

   The Post Office ....

2. A lot of customers have savings accounts at the Post Office.

   There are ....

3. It is cheaper to send things by sea than by airmail.

   It costs ....

4. Valuable or urgent parcels can be posted by special service.

   You ....

5. Parcels must be wrapped carefully and tied with string.

   You ....

Part 2 Questions 6–15 You and two friends are going to spend a few days in another city. You have received a form to book hotel rooms by post. Fill in the form below, giving details about yourself and the rooms you and your friends require. You can use this page for your rough answer but you must write your final answer on your answer sheet.

Bridge Hotel

Reservation Form

Name (6) .... *Mr/Mrs/Miss/Ms
                                    (*please delete)

Nationality (7) ....

Address (8) ....

....

....

Daytime Telephone No (9) ....

Rooms required (10) ....

Number of nights (11) ....

Check in date (12) ....

How will you get here? (13) ....

Meals required (14) ....

Signature (15) ....

Part 3 You have just spent the weekend away from home. Write a letter of about 100 words to an English-speaking friend, telling him/her about three things you did. You can use ideas from some of the pictures below to help you. You can use this sheet for your rough answers but you must write your final answer on the back of your answer sheet.

Dear

I've just had a fantastic weekend away! ....

....

....

....

....

....

....

....

....

....

....

....

....

....

Listening

PART 1

Explanation

You can answer the Listening test on the test paper, but at the end of the test you have to transfer your answers to Parts 1, 2, 3 and 4 onto an answer sheet. You will have 12 minutes to transfer your answers.

In Part 1 you will hear seven short recordings. Sometimes only one person is speaking, but usually there are two speakers. For each of the recordings, there is a set of four pictures. As you listen to each one you must choose the picture which best matches what the speakers say and put a tick (✓) in the correct box. This exercise tests your ability to recognize words and understand how they are being used in a sentence. You will hear each recording twice so that you can check your choice of picture.

Preparation

Exercise 1 🔲

Look at these pictures. Working in pairs, find the pictures that match these key words or expressions.

| by bus | with short sleeves | at half past four | not open yet | in town | in a hurry |

1 a ☐   b ☐

2 a ☐   b ☐

3 a ☐   b ☐

4 a ☐   b ☐

5 a ☐   b ☐

6 a ☐   b ☐

Discuss which key words you could use to describe the other pictures. Then listen to the cassette and match the pictures with the dialogues 1–6.

Exercise 2

Working in pairs, look at the vocabulary below and check that you both know what all the words mean.

> calendar   light bulb   armchair   drawer
> chest of drawers   ashtray   cigarette   wall
> wastepaper basket   teapot   cushion   floor
> switch [on/off]   television set   cassette recorder

Student A Look at picture 1 on page 111.
Student B Look at picture 3 on page 112.
Each describe your picture to your partner and make a list of the differences between the two pictures.

Exercise 3

Look at the maps (**A–D**). Then read the dialogue and decide which map the dialogue refers to.

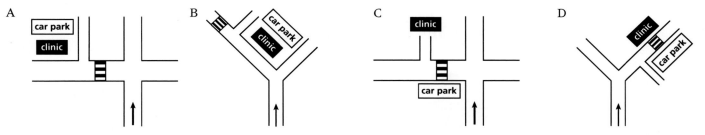

A   Excuse me. Is there anywhere around here where I can park my car?
B   Yes. Turn left at the fork in the road, then turn right just before you get to the zebra crossing. The car park's at the back of the clinic.

Look at the expressions below. Then, working in pairs, make similar dialogues for the other three diagrams.

> **Useful expressions:**
> opposite   on the corner of   between   behind   next to
> in front of   on the left   on the right   straight ahead
> turn left   turn right   at the side of   at the back of

Exercise 4

Which of these pictures (**A–D**) does the dialogue refer to?

A   B   C   D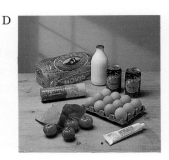

A Did you manage to get everything on my list?

B I think so. Let's see ... a bottle of milk, two cans of soft drinks, a packet of biscuits, a loaf of bread, a dozen eggs, half a kilo of tomatoes, and a tube of toothpaste. That's everything, isn't it?

Working in pairs, make similar dialogues for the other three pictures.

Exercise 5

Which of these people (**A–D**) is the dialogue describing?

A   B   C   D

A How will I recognize Mr Jones when I meet him?

B Well, he's about six foot tall, and thin. He's bald, and he has a fair moustache.
He has a dark blue suit on and he's carrying a white raincoat and a light-coloured case.

Look at the vocabulary below. Then, working in pairs, make similar dialogues about the other three men.

Useful vocabulary:
straight   curly   wide   narrow   beard
moustache   fair   dark   bald   glasses   jacket
trousers   long/short hair   broad shoulders

Exercise 6 📼

Look again at the pictures in Exercises 3, 4 and 5. Listen and decide which picture each dialogue on the cassette refers to.

1 ☐   2 ☐   3 ☐

Test practice   **Part 1 Questions 1–7** Put a tick in the box you think is the most suitable.

Example:

A ✓   B ☐   C ☐   D ☐

1.

A ☐   B ☐   C ☐   D ☐

2.

A ☐   B ☐   C ☐   D ☐

3.

A ☐   B ☐   C ☐   D ☐

4.

A ☐   B ☐   C ☐   D ☐

5.

A ☐   B ☐   C ☐   D ☐

6.

A ☐   B ☐   C ☐   D ☐

7.

A ☐

B ☐

C ☐

D ☐

PART 2

Explanation　For Part 2 you will hear some information about either a place, an event, or an activity. There is only one person speaking and the information often includes details about dates, times, facilities, travel, etc. There are six short questions, with four possible answers for each one. The questions test your ability to recognize pieces of information. As you listen to the recording you must choose the correct answer and tick (✓) the box (**A**, **B**, **C** or **D**) next to it. You will hear the recording twice.

Preparation　### Exercise 1

In Exercise 2 you are going to listen to Sharon describing her school uniform. But first look at questions 1–4 and try to predict Sharon's answer to each question. The first one has been done for you as an example.

1　What are your school colours?

Our school colours are...

2　What kind of shirts do you wear?

3　When do you wear tracksuits?

4　When was the school uniform designed?

Exercise 2

Now listen to the recording and put a tick in the box next to the right answer.

1　What are the school colours?
   A　blue and grey ☐
   B　green and yellow ☐
   C　brown and red ☐
   D　grey and green ☐

2　What kind of shirts do they wear?
   A　blue with long sleeves ☐
   B　grey with long sleeves ☐
   C　blue with short sleeves ☐
   D　white with short sleeves ☐

3　When do they wear tracksuits?
   A　for travelling ☐
   B　on Saturdays ☐
   C　all the time ☐
   D　for games ☐

4　When was the school uniform designed?
   A　in 1960 ☐
   B　in 1986 ☐
   C　in 1966 ☐
   D　in 1916 ☐

Exercise 3

In the recording in Exercise 2, Sharon gave some information that was not necessary to answer the questions. It is useful to look at the questions carefully, so that you know exactly what information to listen for. Read questions 1–5, then look at the list (a–r) which follows.

ENTERTAINMENT GUIDE

1 Exhibitions starting this week:
   A railway posters ☐
   B model boats ☐
   C toys ☐
   D modern paintings ☐

2 Arts Centre special feature:
   A opera ☐
   B new play ☐
   C classical music ☐
   D film ☐

3 Reservations can be made through:
   A Tourist centre ☐
   B Arts Centre ☐
   C cinema ☐
   D post office ☐

4 Tourist Centre open:
   A every day ☐
   B Mon–Sat ☐
   C Mon–Fri ☐
   D Tues–Sat ☐

5 Next month's attractions:
   A opera ☐
   B fun fair ☐
   C circus ☐
   D pop concert ☐

Now that you have read the questions, decide which of the topics on this list you need to find out about when you listen.

a different kinds of sports
b different kinds of exhibitions
c opening times of exhibitions
d names of films
e opening times of Arts Centre
f telephone numbers
g addresses
h what's on next week
i what's on next month
j dates of exhibition
k name of opera
l times of day
m days of week
n names of cinemas
o names of actors
p booking times
q booking offices
r different kinds of entertainment

Exercise 4 🖭

Look at the Entertainment Guide in Exercise 3. Listen to the cassette and put a tick in the box next to the right answer (A, B, C or D). To help you, the recording has been divided into sections.

Test practice   **Part 2 Questions 8–13** Put a tick in the box you think is the most suitable.

SCHOOL TRIP

8 How long will the trip last?
   A One day ☐
   B Two days ☐
   C A week ☐
   D Two weeks ☐

9 Which of these clothes are not mentioned?
   A Sweater ☐
   B Jeans ☐
   C Socks ☐
   D Gloves ☐

10 Why are strong sensible shoes necessary?
   A For running ☐
   B For walking ☐
   C For driving ☐
   D For climbing ☐

11 What should you take if you want to go swimming?
   A A towel and a swimming costume ☐
   B A swimming costume ☐
   C Two towels and a swimming costume ☐
   D A swimming costume, towel and spare socks ☐

12 What's going to happen in the evening?
   A A disco and then a meal ☐
   B A walk and then a disco ☐
   C Either a disco or a meal ☐
   D A meal and then a disco ☐

13 What kind of clothes should be worn in the evening?
   A Cool ☐
   B Warm ☐
   C Comfortable ☐
   D Loose ☐

PART 3

Explanation For Part 3 you will hear a recording where one person is speaking. Occasionally, the recording may include an introduction by a second speaker, such as the beginning of an interview. You need to select specific information from what you hear in order to complete a form or a set of notes. There are six questions and you should write a few words or numbers in each space. You will hear the recording twice.

Preparation **Exercise 1**

Make lists, putting each of the words below into the correct category.

pound	August	hour	ounce	third	gram	March	Sunday	second
fourth	year	inch	April	feet	January	fifth	centimetre	month
pence	second	minute	first	February	Thursday	kilogram	Wednesday	
Monday	July	pound	June	yard	November	metre		

days and dates	length of time	length (measurement)	money	weight
fourth	hour	inch	pence	kilogram

Look at the following abbreviations. Write them next to the words they refer to on your lists.

p   lb   oz   5th   sec

Jan   2nd   cm   ft   Wed

Exercise 2 📼

Listen to the dialogues (1–9) and write in the missing information. Use numbers and abbreviations where you can. The first one has been done for you.

EXAMPLE 1 time: ...*2.30.*.............. 4 price: .... 7 months: ....

2 date: .... 5 breakfast from: ...... to: .... 8 population: ....

3 weight: .... 6 width: .... 9 distance: ....

Exercise 3 📼

You are going to listen to a weather forecast. Before you listen, look at the weather forecast for Monday (below). Fill in the gaps with items from this list.

cloudy	5°	5 Feb	east

WEATHER FORECAST

Date: Monday, ...

	day	night
weather conditions	..............., heavy rain later	snow
temperature	.... –7°C	0°–2°C
wind direction	light south-east	light ....

Now listen to the cassette. You will hear the forecast for Monday first. Check that your answers are correct. Then listen to the forecasts for Tuesday and Wednesday and complete the table.

Date: *Tuesday, 6th February*	day	night
weather conditions	*sunny, cloudy later*	
temperature		*below 0°C*
wind direction		*calm*
Date:	day	night
weather conditions		
temperature		*4°–6°C*
wind direction	*light west*	

Test practice   **Part 3 Questions 14–19** Look at the notes about Annabel Green. Some
information is missing. For each question, fill in the missing information in the
numbered space.

Name: .... *Annabel Green* ....

Work: .... *Artist* ....

Place of work: (14) ....

Hours of work: (15) ....

Likes: (16) ....

Dislikes: (17) ....

Place of exhibition: (18) ....

Dates and times: (19) ....

PART 4

Explanation For Part 4 you will hear a conversation between two people. They are discussing a subject they are both interested in, and they may agree or disagree with each other. You will read six short sentences about the conversations. You must decide whether the sentences are correct or not and then tick (✓) the appropriate boxes (**A** or **B**). The questions test your understanding of what the conversation is about, and also your understanding of the speakers' attitudes and opinions. You will hear the recording twice.

Preparation ## Exercise 1 🔲

On the cassette you will hear twelve different people who were asked what they thought about a speech they had just heard. The speech was against some plans to build a new motorway.
Listen and fill in the table, putting a tick (✓) to show whether the speakers liked or disliked the speech. Remember that the tone of voice is important, as well as the words. It will help you to decide what the speakers are thinking.

	speaker											
	1	2	3	4	5	6	7	8	9	10	11	12
liked the speech	✓											
disliked the speech		✓										

Exercise 2

Sometimes you will need to decide if the speakers are agreeing or disagreeing with each other. Look at the expressions in the table. Put a tick to show if they express agreement or disagreement.

	agreement	disagreement
1 Yes, you're probably right.	✓	
2 Are you sure about that?		✓
3 That's a good idea.		
4 I see what you mean.		
5 I'm afraid I can't support you there.		
6 I doubt it.		
7 That's impossible.		
8 Nobody could argue with that.		
9 Just a moment – that's not right.		
10 I refuse to believe that.		

Exercise 3 🔲

Look at the pictures 1–10 and listen to the ten short conversations. Decide whether the speakers are agreeing or disagreeing. Put a tick (✓) if you think they are agreeing and a cross (✗) if you think they are disagreeing.

Exercise 4

Sometimes when you listen, you need to match a statement with the correct part of the conversation. This may seem difficult if the conversation is quite long. Read the conversation below, then look at questions 1–7 on page 72.

Write the key words (in *italics*) in the conversation under the statements they refer to. The first one has been done for you.

		A	B
EXAMPLE	1 In the end, the woman has persuaded the man to change his mind about the interview.	☐	☐

I still don't think

2   The man is looking forward to his interview.   ☐ ☐

....

3   He would have to spend three months travelling abroad every year.   ☐ ☐

....

4   The woman thinks that he will get the job.   ☐ ☐

....

5   The woman was impressed by the man's German.   ☐ ☐

....

6   The man really wants the job.   ☐ ☐

....

7   The man feels confident about his ability to speak foreign languages.   ☐ ☐

....

Without reading the conversation again, listen to the cassette and tick the boxes next to questions 1–7. Tick the box under A if you agree with the statement. If you do not agree, put a tick in the box under B.

Test practice   **Part 4 Questions 20–25** If you agree with the statement, put a tick in the box under **A**. If you do **not** agree, put a tick in the box under **B**.

	A	B
20. The man wears jeans every day.	☐	☐
21. The woman agrees that the man should wear his jeans.	☐	☐
22. The woman wants to wear a red dress.	☐	☐
23. The man likes the red dress.	☐	☐
24. They both think there will be a lot of people at the party.	☐	☐
25. In the end, the man and the woman agree about what they should wear for the party.	☐	☐

Listening test

Part 1 Questions 1–7 Put a tick in the box you think is the most suitable.

Example:

£415	£115	£450	£150
A ☐	B ✓	C ☐	D ☐

1.
A ☐   B ☐   C ☐   D ☐

2.
A ☐   B ☐   C ☐   D ☐

3.
A ☐   B ☐   C ☐   D ☐

4.

A ☐   B ☐   C ☐   D ☐

5.

A ☐   B ☐   C ☐   D ☐

6.

A ☐   B ☐   C ☐   D ☐

7.

A ☐   B ☐   C ☐   D ☐

Part 2 Questions 8–13 Put a tick in the box you think is the most suitable.

TRAFFIC CONDITIONS

8 Traffic is held up on the way to the airport because of

A ice on the road. ☐

B fog in the valley. ☐

C darkness. ☐

D bright sunlight. ☐

9 In the river valley it is dangerous to

A ride a bike. ☐

B use your brakes. ☐

C overtake. ☐

D take a rest. ☐

10 In the accident

A many people died. ☐

B half the people were alive. ☐

C no one was left alive. ☐

D no people died. ☐

11 Near Kingsgate police station there's a speed limit of

A 30 miles per hour. ☐

B 15 miles per hour. ☐

C 20 miles per hour. ☐

D 25 miles per hour. ☐

12 The hovercraft departure is

A on time. ☐

B delayed. ☐

C put off until later. ☐

D closed. ☐

13 If you are going for a walk in the dark you should

A ride a bike. ☐

B wear bright clothes. ☐

C stay in the house. ☐

D go over the road. ☐

Part 3 Questions 14–19 Look at the notes about the students' centre. Some information is missing. For each question, fill in the missing information in the numbered space.

STUDENTS' CENTRE

What the centre has to offer

Shop – sells food and (14) ....

Laundry – for washing and (15) ....

Clinic – has a doctor, a nurse and a (16) ....

　　　　　Emergency number (nights only): (17) ....

Advice centre – run by (18) ....

Where to find the centre

New building, near the (19) ....

Part 4 Questions 20–25 If you agree with the statement, put a tick in the box under **A**. If you do **not** agree, put a tick in the box under **B**.

		A	B
20.	The man is going on holiday next month.	☐	☐
21.	The man is looking forward to his holiday.	☐	☐
22.	At first, the woman thinks the man is ill.	☐	☐
23.	The man is afraid of catching a disease from an insect bite.	☐	☐
24.	The woman thinks the man is right to feel afraid of getting ill.	☐	☐
25.	In the end, the man realizes that his fears are mistaken.	☐	☐

Speaking

The PET Speaking test lasts between 10 and 12 minutes and there are four Parts. You take the Speaking test in pairs, with two examiners present. During the interview, one of the examiners will make some notes and write on a marksheet. The other examiner will begin each Part and help the two candidates in their discussion. (Sometimes the Speaking test is taken by groups of three candidates.)

PART 1

Explanation

In Part 1 you will be asked some questions such as your name and candidate number, your address, where you come from, etc. You may be asked to spell your name or part of your address. You will score higher marks if you can introduce one or two of your own ideas to the conversation as well as answer the examiner's questions accurately. Part 1 lasts about 2 minutes.

Preparation

Exercise 1

Match the questions and answers in this interview. Then number them (1–10) to show the correct order of the conversation. The first one has been done for you, as an example.

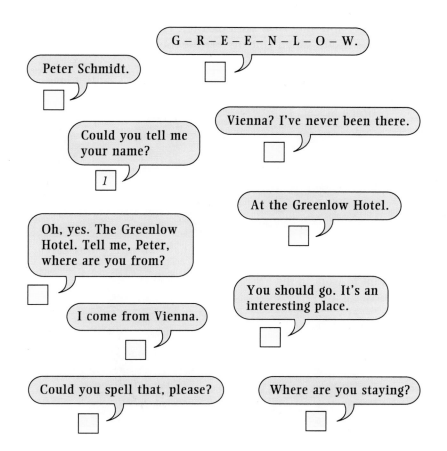

Exercise 2

One of the things the interviewer said to Peter was not a question, but Peter replied.

Vienna? I've never been there.

You should go. It's an interesting place.

Working in pairs, tell your partner about your home town, using some of the sentences below.

It's a ... place.　　　　　　　　　　　　It's famous for ...
It's an exciting place to live because ...　　A lot of people visit it, because ...
It's only a small town, but ...　　　　　　Not many people visit it, because ...

Working in pairs, discuss how many ways you can find to complete these sentences.

1　It usually takes ... to get to school	by ... on ...
2　I have to set off ... but it takes less time if ...	
3　I've always dreamt about ...	
4　I'm very fond of ... 　I'm fairly good at ...	so ...

Now look at the pictures below of an interview. In pairs, take turns to play the part of the interviewer and interview your partner. The sentences you have just practised may be useful when you answer the interviewer.

Exercise 3

The interviewer may ask you to spell words and give numbers. Look at the dialogue below, then, in pairs, make similar dialogues using the other cards.

The Cornucopia Restaurant

160 Belvedere Avenue
Tel: 356 9344

Eezeequick
Dry Cleaning

Box 1066
Hastings
Tel: 90771

Frederick W. Kosofsky
Manager
Sales Department

Excalibur Oil Company
Tel: 0540 662299

Rivermead Garage

20 Sylvester Square
Tel: 105772 (daytime)
Emergency: 114750

Dialogue:

A What's the name of the restaurant in Belvedere Avenue?
B The Cornucopia.
A Could you spell that, please?
B C-O-R-N-U-C-O-P-I-A.
A Thanks. What's the telephone number?
B Three five six, nine three four four.

Look at the four business cards again and listen to the telephone calls on the cassette. Decide whether the information given is right or wrong.

EXAMPLE 1 *right* ....

2 ....

3 ....

4 ....

5 ....

6 ....

Exercise 4

The interviewer will try to encourage you to speak. You should try to avoid giving one-word answers. Look at these questions and answers. Make notes to expand the answers. Then, working in pairs, ask and answer the questions. The first one has been done for you as an example.

EXAMPLE

1 Have you always lived here?
   Yes. *I was born here. My parents moved here fifteen years ago.*
   No. *I came here when I was twelve.*
2 Do you often come to this part of town?
   Yes. ...
   No. ...
3 Is your school far from here?
   Yes. ...
   No. ...
4 Does your elder brother live at home?
   Yes. ...
   No. ...
5 Do you like sports?
   Yes. ...
   No. ...
6 Do you travel a lot?
   Yes. ...
   No. ...
7 Have you got a favourite subject at school?
   Yes. ...
   No. ...
8 Is there anything special that you like doing at the weekend?
   Yes. ...
   No. ...

Exercise 5

Listen to the questions on the cassette. Put a tick in the box next to the right answer for each one.

1 ☐ OK.
  ☐ I can.
  ☐ Yes, thank you.

2 ☐ No, not very long. Only a few minutes.
  ☐ It was ten minutes to eleven.
  ☐ I was waiting outside the room.

3 ☐ I don't know the exact time.
  ☐ It was just starting to rain.
  ☐ Yes, I like this kind of weather very much.

4 ☐ Including my own language? Three altogether.
  ☐ I've been studying English for four years.
  ☐ No, I can't speak it very well.

5 ☐ It's about one kilometre.
  ☐ Yes, it's very far away.
  ☐ For more than five kilometres.

6 ☐ I'll take the bus to my school.
  ☐ Yes, I sometimes miss the bus.
  ☐ At the bus stop opposite the bank.

Exercise 6

If you don't hear or understand the question, ask the speaker to repeat it. Don't just sit and say nothing!

Listen to this conversation. There is a lot of noise going on, so the student has to repeat what she has said. Write down the expressions that the woman uses to get her to repeat what she has just said. You should be able to find six. The first one has been done for you.

EXAMPLE 1 *I'm sorry, I didn't hear that.* ...... 4 ......

2 ...... 5 ......

3 ...... 6 ......

Test practice Part 1

1. Pretend you don't know your partner. Prepare some questions:
   1. about your partner's name.
   2. about your partner's home address. (Ask your partner to spell something or give a number.)
   3. about the way your partner came here.
   4. about your partner's home town.

2. Ask your partner the questions you have prepared.

PART 2

Explanation   In Part 2 the examiner will explain that he/she is going to describe a situation to you and will then give the two of you a picture to look at. You will have a few seconds to think about what to say in such a situation and the examiner will then offer to repeat the description of the situation if you wish. In this part you often have to give opinions, agree and disagree, make suggestions, etc. Part 2 lasts about 2–3 minutes.

Preparation   ### Exercise 1 🔲

Look at these pictures and listen to the conversation. What do the two students decide to do?

Exercise 2

Match the beginnings and ends of these questions and statements.

1 ☐ Are you free

2 ☐ Why don't we

3 ☐ I'd rather

4 ☐ What are you

5 ☐ Monday would

6 ☐ What do you think about

a   be better as I don't have to work.

b   going to Spain for our next holiday?

c   go to that new restaurant?

d   on Wednesday evening?

e   doing tomorrow?

f   go another time.

Exercise 3

Now listen again to the dialogue that you heard in Exercise 1 and fill in the missing words.

A What (1) .... this evening?

B (2) .... to see *Hamlet*? I've heard it's really good.

A Oh, I don't know. The last time I went to see a Shakespeare play, I fell asleep.

B Really? This production is set in this century, and they say it's quite unusual.
      I suppose (3) .... to the disco or a restaurant (4) ....

A (5) .... Certainly not the disco, anyway. The music was
      awful last time we went.

B Well, (6) ....?

A I think the others in the class (7) ....
      to see the film at the Odeon – it's that new thriller that everyone's talking
      about. What do you think? Would you like to go?

B Oh yes. (8) ....! Let's see what the others think.

Exercise 4

Work in pairs. Discuss the activities mentioned in Exercise 1 and decide which
one you would like to do.

Exercise 5

Look at the following sentences. Two people are trying to arrange an evening out. Reorder the sentences to make their conversation. The first one has been done for you.

☐ **A** Sure. I'll call and book now.

☐ **B** Yes, I think so. It'll be busy so we'd better book. What time shall we go?

☐ **A** Fine. Are you doing anything on Wednesday evening?

☐ **B** Good idea! What kind of food do you like?

1 **A** Let's go out for a meal one day this week.

☐ **B** Can we make it 8.30?

☐ **A** Anything really. Do you like Thai food?

☐ **B** Yes, I have to work late. The end of the week's probably better for me.

☐ **A** Are you free on Friday?

☐ **A** 8 o'clock?

☐ **B** I love it. We could try that new Thai restaurant in James Street.

Exercise 6

Work in pairs. You want to hire a video to watch together sometime next week. Read through your instructions and act out the dialogue. Choose from the following kinds of video.

Thriller   Musical   Comedy   Science Fiction   Horror

Student A
Ask B what kind of video he/she would like to watch.

Student B

Say what kind of video you would prefer to watch.

Disagree. Say why.

Suggest another kind of video. Try to get your partner to agree.

Agree. Suggest the name of a film.

Disagree and say why. Suggest another film.

Agree.

Try to arrange a time to see it.

Disagree and say why.

Suggest a different time to see it.

Agree.

Now change roles and try the conversation again. Choose different videos this time.

Test practice   Part 2

It's your teacher's birthday. You and your partner would like to get her/him a present. Talk about the items below and choose one of them.

Think about the following questions:
What kind?   How many?   How much?

PART 3

Explanation

Parts 3 and 4 are linked together. In Part 3 the examiner will give each of you another picture, probably a colour photograph, and ask you to describe or talk about it in detail. In Part 4 the examiner will encourage you to talk more generally using the picture from Part 3 as a starting point. You may be asked about your opinions or experiences, what you like or dislike, etc. Parts 3 and 4 last about 5 minutes in total.

Preparation

Exercise 1

Look at the photograph below. In pairs, complete the three tables about the background, the people and the action in the picture. If you are sure about your answer, put it in the column under 'definitely'. If you are not sure, put it under 'probably'. The first one has been done for you as an example.

Table 1: Background

	definitely	**probably**
place	a station	
town or country		country or a small town
season		
weather		
time of day		

Table 2: People

	definitely	**probably**
how many		
ages		
occupations		
clothes		
mood		

Table 3: Action

	definitely	**probably**
moving		
preparing to		
holding		

Exercise 2

In the tables in Exercise 1, when you have put something in the 'definitely' column you are sure about it. Look at the examples below of talking about things you are sure about. Then, working in pairs, see how many sentences like these you can make about the picture.

EXAMPLES   *It's a station. But it's definitely not an ordinary station because it's such a tiny train.*

You can tell the people on the platform are ... because ...

They must be ... because ...

It can't be very cold because ...

Exercise 3

The examiner will expect you to make guesses in this part of the test. In the tables in Exercise 1, you are making a guess when you have put something in the 'probably' column. Look at the examples below of making guesses. Then in pairs, talk about the things in the picture that you are not sure about.

EXAMPLES

I think he's the engine driver because ...

I don't think it's very hot because ...

I think it might be summer, because the people seem to be ...

It's probably in the country, because ...

I'm only guessing, but I think ...

I'm not sure, but I think ...

Exercise 4

Look at this picture. Working in pairs, use the table below to find as many ways as possible to identify different people and things in the picture.

EXAMPLES

The woman on the right, with her back to us ...

The building which is straight ahead, at the far end of the street ...

The person The man The woman The child	in on with	the ...	
	who	is	...ing
The building	which		

Exercise 5

Look at this picture. Read the examples then, working in pairs, compare the people and things in this picture in as many ways as you can.

EXAMPLES   *The woman on the left seems to be the oldest.*

The boy in the yellow shorts is smaller than the rest.

The car on the right isn't as ... as ...

Exercise 6

Student A   Look at picture 2 on page 111.

Student B   Look at picture 4 on page 112.

Each describe your picture to your partner and make a list of ten differences between the two pictures.

Test practice   **Part 3** Look at your picture and talk about it with your partner.

Picture for Student A

Picture for Student B

PART 4

See explanation on page 86.

Preparation

Exercise 1

The examiner will ask you questions about your own likes and dislikes, experiences and habits, based on the picture in Part 3. Now look at these pictures and match the questions (a–g) to the right pictures.

1

2

3

a Are you a good swimmer? ….
b Do you often go shopping? ….
c What's your favourite kind of food? ….
d Do you have any pets? ….
e Are you interested in water sports? ….
f How do you keep fit? ….
g Are you interested in animals? ….

Exercise 2 📼

It does not matter if you answer 'no' to these questions in the examination, but if the answer is 'no', you should explain why.

Listen to the cassette and match the answers you hear to the questions (a–g) in Exercise 1.

EXAMPLE   a   Are you a good swimmer? *..1..*

Exercise 3

Fill in the table about your own attitudes to different activities. Put a tick to show your answer.

	like	dislike
outdoor sports		
water sports		
do-it-yourself		
visiting the countryside		
animals		
shopping		
travelling		
cycling		
parties		
visiting museums		
gardening		
dancing		
music		
cookery		

Now look at the examples of questions you can ask. Then, in pairs, ask your partner questions and talk about the activities in the table.

EXAMPLES   *Are you good at ...?*

How often ...?

What kind of ... do you enjoy?

Is ... very popular in your country?

How long have you ...?

Why do you/don't you ...?

Test practice   **Part 4** Look at the picture of a picnic, then, working in pairs, answer the questions about it. Make your answers as full as possible.

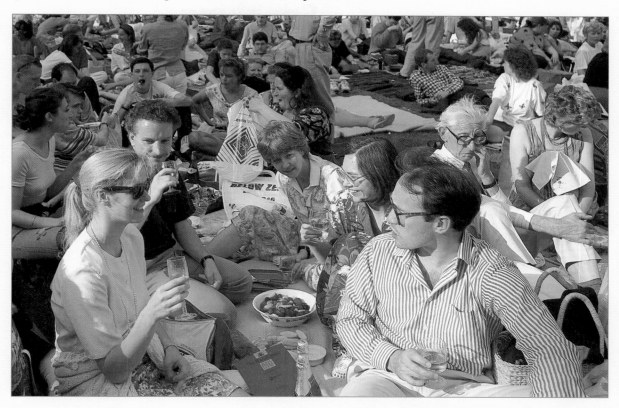

Do you like picnics?   What kind of food do you take with you?
How often do you go on picnics?   Where is your favourite place for a picnic?

Speaking test (page 107)   **Part 3** Student B look at this picture and talk about it with your partner.

Speaking test

Part 1 Pretend you don't know each other. Interview your partner about:

1.   Your partner's family (ages, jobs, where they live, their interests).

2.   Your partner's education (schools attended, past and present; favourite subjects; future plans).

Part 2 You and your partner have the opportunity to go on one of the following courses this weekend. Talk about the different courses and decide which you would like to do.

windsurfing   photography   mountain walking
drawing and painting

Part 3 Look at your picture and talk about it with your partner.

Picture for Student A

Picture for Student B

Part 4 Talk to your partner about what kind of work you would like to do. Do the activities in the pictures attract you? Give reasons why/why not. Would you be any good at the activities shown in the pictures?

Practice test paper

READING AND WRITING TEST (*time allowed: 1½ hours*)

Part 1 Questions 1–5 Look at the five pictures of signs below. Someone asks you what each sign means. For each sign, mark the correct letter – **A**, **B**, **C** or **D** – on your answer sheet.

Example:

Part 1				
O	A ■	B □	C □	D □

1.

    A   There is a new lift and stairs.

    B   You can't use the lift at present, but you can use the stairs.

    C   You can use either the lift or the stairs.

    D   There is now a lift available instead of stairs.

2.

    A   The office will open before ten o'clock if you ring the bell.

    B   After ten o'clock, ring the bell and someone will see you.

    C   The office is only open at ten o'clock. You should make an appointment by phone.

    D   You can go into the office before ten o'clock if you have an appointment.

3.

    A   The entrance to the building is the second door on the right.

    B   This is not the correct way to get into the building.

    C   This is not the main entrance to the building.

    D   The car park is on the right hand side of the building.

4.

    A   Smoking in this area can damage your health.

    B   You are advised to stop smoking if you enter this area.

    C   If you go past this place, you must not smoke.

    D   You cannot smoke here, but smoking is allowed further on.

5.

A   This week kitchen furniture will be £5 cheaper.

B   After this week, kitchen furniture will cost £5.

C   The price of kitchen furniture will be reduced next week.

D   Special kitchen furniture is only available for one week.

Part 2 Questions 6–10 The following people all want to go on holiday. Look at the advertisements for holidays, and decide which holiday would be best for each person. Mark the correct letter – **A** to **H** – on your answer sheet.

Example:

Part 2								
O	A	B	C	D	E	F	G	H
	■	☐	☐	☐	☐	☐	☐	☐

6.   John and Samantha are university students. They want to have a holiday in the summer, but they have very little money.

7.   Peter Brown is a businessman. He is tired and needs a rest but he does not have very much free time for a holiday. He wants to get away from city life and stay somewhere near the sea.

8.   The Robinson family, Mr and Mrs Robinson and their twins, aged 11, like outdoor holidays. They have never tried sailing, but they would like to learn.

9.   Susan James has three weeks to spend on holiday. She doesn't like sports, but she doesn't like relaxing on a beach either. She enjoys sightseeing and learning about foreign countries.

10.   Bill Jones is 30. He wants an active, exciting holiday. He likes hot weather but he doesn't like the sea.

A   Explore Africa
Do you like adventure? Are you looking for a holiday you will never forget? Travel through Africa for five weeks with a small group. Groups fly to Nairobi every Saturday, starting May 24th. If you are aged 25–45 send now for a brochure to Box 342.

B   Exciting Holiday Camp
Climb, sail and swim taught by trained adults in a camp near a lake. All meals provided. Camps throughout June, July and August, each lasting for two weeks. Boys and girls aged 9–14.

C   Seagull Sailing Holidays
Suitable for all ages. Learn to sail in three weeks. Teaching from qualified staff, no experience necessary. Accommodation is provided in holiday flats in a beautiful quiet fishing village. Breakfast, dinner and a packed lunch included in the price of the holiday.

D   Bell Island Hotel
Short stays (3–7 days) available. Famous for its excellent cooking, the hotel provides opportunities to relax and enjoy the heated swimming pool, the disco and top class bar and restaurants with entertainment every night. All rooms have sea views. Special reduced prices in winter months (November–March).

E   History Tours
Tour Egypt with guides. The tour includes lectures about the history of Egypt and visits to museums. Travel by coach or river boat. Accommodation in top hotels. Tours last 2–3 weeks.

F   City Tours
Travel by air to Paris, Amsterdam, Vienna or Rome. Three or four day stays in city centre hotels. Bed and breakfast only. There are guides available in each place to show you around the city. Tours and theatre tickets available at extra cost.

G   Students' Working Holidays
For a really cheap (but healthy!) holiday. Pick fruit in the heart of the country. Accommodation provided in farmhouses or camp in tents. All meals included. Free transport to place of work from railway station. If you are over sixteen, why not write for further details?

H   Caribbean Island Holidays
Sail among the islands on board a beautiful sailing boat. The boat has everything you could wish for on this perfect holiday among the islands of the Caribbean. Enjoy a lazy holiday in the sun – the holiday of your dreams. Each trip lasts two weeks.

Part 3 Questions 11–20 Below is some information about restaurants. Check the notes you have been given against the text. Mark **A** on your answer sheet if you think the notes are correct and mark **B** if you think the notes are incorrect.

Example:

Part 3		
O	A ▄	B ☐

11. All the restaurants serve breakfast.

12. Some of the restaurants are closed on Mondays.

13. Kathy's Kitchen would be a good place to have dinner.

14. Only one restaurant says you must book in advance.

15. Three of the restaurants offer special lunches.

16. All the restaurants are open on Sundays.

17. Jackson's Restaurant is the most suitable for children.

18. Some of the restaurants are closed in the middle of the afternoon.

19. Mr Beefy stays open the longest.

20. Two of the restaurants advertise light meals.

Where to Eat in Springhill

Chopsticks Chinese Restaurant

The only Chinese restaurant
in Springville.
Open for lunch and dinner
Tuesday – Sunday (closed Mondays)
Special Business lunch menu
includes six different main courses.
Special prices for groups of ten or more.

Kathy's Kitchen

*Home-cooked snacks served
from 10.00 – 5.30.
Meet your friends and enjoy
our soups and salads, home-
made cakes and biscuits.
We can also organise
children's birthday parties.*

Mr Beefy Hamburger Restaurant

Quick meals and snacks
for all the family.
Enjoy our famous hamburgers –
choose from twelve different kinds.
Open 9.00 a.m. to midnight all week.

The Windmill Family Restaurant

Our speciality – children's parties.
Babies welcome. Special shopper's
lunch on Fridays and Saturdays.
Open 12.30 – 8.00 p.m. daily.
Sunday 11.30 a.m. – 5.00 p.m.

Jackson's Restaurant

Superb fresh fish and seafood, cooked by
our French chef. Excellent wine list.
Open for lunch 12.00 p.m.–3.00 p.m.
Dinner 6.30 p.m.–midnight.
Closed Sundays and Mondays
Reservations necessary.

Part 4 Questions 21–25 Read this passage and then answer the questions below. Mark the correct letter – **A**, **B**, **C** or **D** – on your answer sheet.

Example:

What is life like for today's students? As the university and college terms began, I talked to a few students about their lives.

Sarah James is a second year biology student. 'Money is a big problem,' said Sarah. 'I can eat quite cheaply at the university, but I spend quite a lot on transport. I also spend quite a lot on clothes, as I like to wear things that are in fashion.'

Colin Peters, who is studying engineering, disagrees. 'I don't spend anything on clothes,' he said, 'unless you count climbing boots. I'm very keen on climbing, and you do need special equipment, some of which is very expensive. Luckily, my parents gave me money for my birthday in November. Not much of my money goes on transport, because I have a bicycle.'

Diana Bell is a first year fashion student. 'I make all my own clothes. This should save me money, but in fact, the materials are very expensive. I don't know how I would manage if I didn't sell some of the dresses and hats I make to the other students. Everything is expensive,' she said. 'That includes the rent, food, transport and heating for the flat in winter.'

Jack is a science student in his final year. 'What do I spend my money on? Well, not on clothes, and not a lot on going out in the evening. My rent is expensive, and I suppose I spend quite a lot on books.'

21.   This is from

   A   a student's notebook.

   B   a letter to a friend.

   C   a magazine article.

   D   an advertisement.

22.   The aim of the writer is to

   A   show how students live.

   B   give advice to students.

   C   explain that students work hard.

   D   complain about students' way of life.

23.   The students' main problem is

   A   deciding what to wear.

   B   living on the money they receive.

   C   finding enough time to study.

   D   cooking their own food.

24. Colin is different from Sarah because

    A   he has generous parents who help him.

    B   he doesn't need to study very hard.

    C   he is not a second year student.

    D   his clothes and transport cost less.

25. Which of the following is true for Diana?

    A
    I haven't bought any clothes this year but I will have to next year when I start work.

    B
    I'm going to buy a new pair of boots this winter, after my birthday.

    C
    I bought a new jacket and trousers yesterday, so I haven't any money.

    D
    A friend is going to pay me to make a jacket for her, so I will have enough money after all.

Part 5 Questions 26–35 Read the passage below and mark the correct letter on your answer sheet.

Example:

I am going to a wedding ^{26}.............. Saturday. My great friend, Marie, and her fiancé, George, are ^{27}..............married. They have known each other ^{28}..............five years, but they have only been going out together a short time. I must say, we were all rather ^{29}..............when they announced that they were engaged.

The wedding will be in the church near Marie's parents' home and ^{30}..............there will be a party in the Church Hall. There will be almost a hundred ^{31}..............at the party. Besides both ^{32}..............families, all Marie's friends from college will be at the wedding and Marie and George have also ^{33}..............a lot of people from the office where they both ^{34}.............. .The party should be great fun. There will be lots of food and drink. There is also going to be a band. We all expect that it will go on ^{35}..............late in the evening.

26.	A last	B next	C at	D from
27.	A becoming	B having	C going	D getting
28.	A after	B until	C for .	D before
29.	A please	B surprised	C friendly	D interesting
30.	A afterwards	B yet	C however	D because
31.	A visitors	B guests	C members	D crowds
32.	A couple	B their	C her	D his
33.	A called	B discussed	C met	D invited
34.	A work	B employ	C left	D manage
35.	A during	B after	C until	D while

WRITING

Part 1 Questions 1–5 Here are some sentences about a college. For each question, finish the second sentence so that it means the same as the first. The second sentence is started for you. Write only the missing words on your answer sheet. You may use this page for any rough work.

Example: Details of courses are available from the secretary.

You can *get details of courses from the secretary.* ....

1. The college has a new library with plenty of room to study.

   There ....

2. Six different courses are offered by the science department.

   The science department ....

3. The computer courses are very popular with students from abroad.

   Students from abroad ....

4. The advanced business course lasts longer than the ordinary business course.

   The ordinary ....

5. Successful students will receive a certificate.

   If ....

Part 2 Questions 6–15 Imagine you are going to attend a sports weekend. Fill in the application form below, giving details about yourself. You can use this page for your rough answers but you must write your final answer on your answer sheet.

SPORTS WEEKEND APPLICATION FORM

Name (6) ....*Mr/Mrs/Miss/Ms
(* please delete)

Address (7) ....

....

....

....

....

Tel No ....

Nationality (8) ....

Date of birth (day, month, year) (9) ....

Where do you usually play sports? (10) ....

....

....

Which sport would you like to join in? (11) ....

....

What sports equipment do you need to borrow? (12) ....

....

....

What is your best sport? How long have you been playing? (13) ....

....

Could you help to organize a sport? Which sport could you help with? (14) ....

....

Signature (15) ....

Part 3 Look at the advertisement below. You want to find out about jobs in one of these areas. Write a letter asking for information. Write about 100 words. The address is not necessary. You can use this page for your rough answer, but you must write your final answer on the back of your answer sheet.

Job Information Service

We give help to young people who want to find out what it is like to work in the following areas:

- Television and films
- Travel
- Fashion
- Newspapers and magazines
- Hotels and restaurants
- Education
- The police
- Sport

Just write a short letter to Jim Mitchell, our Chief Information Officer, and tell him your age and interests, what kind of work you are interested in, and why.

Dear ....

I saw your advertisement in the newspaper. ....

....

....

....

....

....

....

....

....

....

....

....

LISTENING TEST (time allowed: 30 minutes + 12 minutes transfer time)

Part 1 Questions 1–7 Put a tick in the box you think is the most suitable.

Example:

A ☐   B ☐   C ✓   D ☐

1.

A ☐   B ☐   C ☐   D ☐

2.

A ☐   B ☐   C ☐   D ☐

3.

A ☐   B ☐   C ☐   D ☐

4.

A ☐   B ☐   C ☐   D ☐

5.

A ☐   B ☐   C ☐   D ☐

6.

A ☐   B ☐   C ☐   D ☐

7.

A ☐   B ☐   C ☐   D ☐

Part 2 Questions 8–13 Put a tick in the boxes you think are most suitable.

SUMMER COURSES IN ENGLISH

8   Some of the conversation classes will be in groups of

   A   3–5. ☐

   B   5. ☐

   C   7–8. ☐

   D   17. ☐

9   There will be new courses in

   A   reading and computers. ☐

   B   reading and writing. ☐

   C   video and computers. ☐

   D   video and reading. ☐

10   Students can take part in sports at

   A   the school. ☐

   B   the sports hall. ☐

   C   the sports centre. ☐

   D   the school field. ☐

11   As a special surprise there will be

   A   a computer course. ☐

   B   a trip to a place of interest. ☐

   C   a video show. ☐

   D   a visit to a TV studio. ☐

12   Some students may be able to

   A   make video films. ☐

   B   give the other students a surprise. ☐

   C   learn to fly a plane. ☐

   D   plan some special visits. ☐

13   Most of the students will stay

   A   at the school. ☐

   B   in flats. ☐

   C   with families. ☐

   D   in their own home. ☐

Part 3 Questions 14–19 Write the information needed below.

AT WALTON'S DEPARTMENT STORE THIS WEEK

Sale of electrical equipment in (14) ....

The electrical equipment on sale includes coffee makers, (15) ....

....

This month in the café there is a (16) ....

There are special offers on (17) .... on the ground floor.

On the second floor you'll find (18) .... , opposite the bookshop.

On the third floor, tennis rackets are reduced by (19) ....

Part 4 Questions 20–25 If you agree with the statement, put a tick in the box under **A**. If you do **not** agree, put a tick in the box under **B**.

		A	B
20.	The man wants to go shopping for paint first.	☐	☐
21.	The woman wants to buy meat last.	☐	☐
22.	The woman wants to go to the market.	☐	☐
23.	The woman hasn't decided what colour paint she wants.	☐	☐
24.	The man thinks that he can choose the paint on his own.	☐	☐
25.	They both agree to go shopping for paint first.	☐	☐

SPEAKING TEST

Part 1 Pretend you don't know each other. Interview your partner about:

1.   Your partner's home (what kind of house, the people who live there, where it is).

2.   Your partner's activities at home (helping in the house, time spent at home, favourite activities).

Part 2 You and your partner have been asked to help organize a surprise birthday party for a student in your class. Talk about how you will organize it and the preparations you will need to make. Include the following points:

place   time   music   food   guests

Part 3 Student A look at this picture and talk about it with your partner. Student B see page 93.

Part 4 Talk to your partner about your interest in music. Can you play a musical instrument? Which? Would you like to be able to play a musical instrument? Why/Why not? What kind of music do you like listening to? Is there any kind of music that you don't like? Give your reasons.

CAMBRIDGE
EXAMINATIONS, CERTIFICATES & DIPLOMAS
ENGLISH AS A FOREIGN LANGUAGE

University of Cambridge
Local Examinations Syndicate
International Examinations

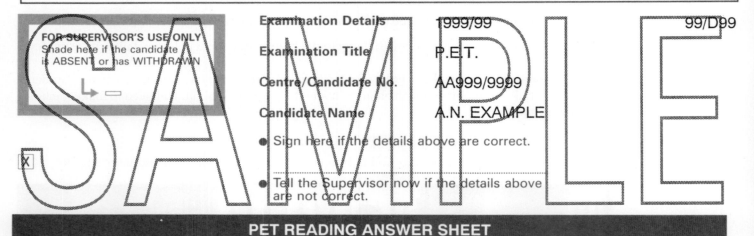

FOR SUPERVISOR'S USE ONLY
Shade here if the candidate
is ABSENT or has WITHDRAWN

Examination Details	1999/99	99/D99
Examination Title	P.E.T.	
Centre/Candidate No.	AA999/9999	
Candidate Name	A.N. EXAMPLE	

● Sign here if the details above are correct.

● Tell the Supervisor now if the details above are not correct.

PET READING ANSWER SHEET

Use a pencil

Mark one letter for each question.

For example:

If you think A is the right answer to the question, mark your answer sheet like this:

Change your answer like this:

Part 1		Part 2		Part 3		Part 4		Part 5	
1	A B C D	**6**	A B C D E F G H	**11**	A B	**21**	A B C D	**26**	A B C D
2	A B C D	**7**	A B C D E F G H	**12**	A B	**22**	A B C D	**27**	A B C D
3	A B C D	**8**	A B C D E F G H	**13**	A B	**23**	A B C D	**28**	A B C D
4	A B C D	**9**	A B C D E F G H	**14**	A B	**24**	A B C D	**29**	A B C D
5	A B C D	**10**	A B C D E F G H	**15**	A B	**25**	A B C D	**30**	A B C D
				16	A B			**31**	A B C D
				17	A B			**32**	A B C D
				18	A B			**33**	A B C D
				19	A B			**34**	A B C D
				20	A B			**35**	A B C D

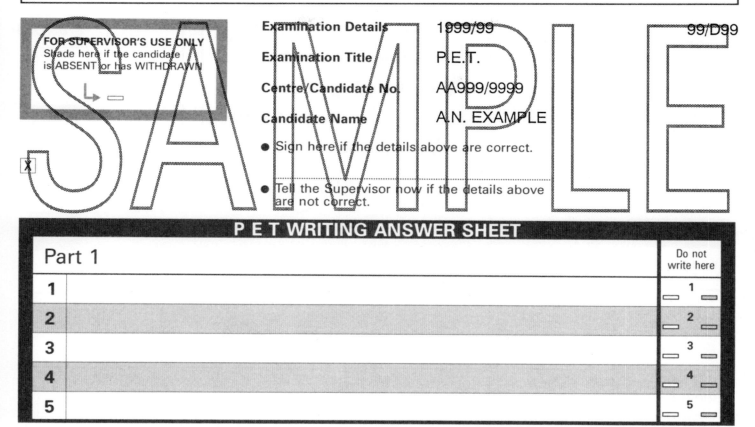

Continue with Part 3 on the other side of this sheet ➔

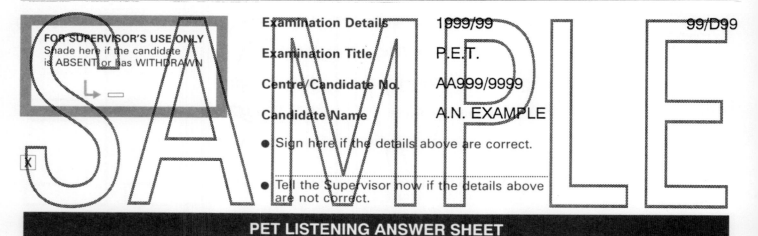

CAMBRIDGE
EXAMINATIONS, CERTIFICATES & DIPLOMAS
ENGLISH AS A FOREIGN LANGUAGE

University of Cambridge
Local Examinations Syndicate
International Examinations

FOR SUPERVISOR'S USE ONLY
Shade here if the candidate
is ABSENT or has WITHDRAWN

Examination Details   1999/99   99/D99

Examination Title   P.E.T.

Centre/Candidate No. AA999/9999

Candidate Name   A.N. EXAMPLE

● Sign here if the details above are correct.

● Tell the Supervisor now if the details above
  are not correct.

PET LISTENING ANSWER SHEET

• You must transfer all your answers from the Listening Question Paper to this answer sheet.

Use a pencil

For Parts 1,2 and 4: Mark one letter for each question.

For example, if you think A is the right answer to
the question, mark your answer sheet like this:

Change your answer
like this:

For Part 3: Write your answers in the spaces
next to the numbers (14 - 19) like this:

0   *example*   ▭ 0 ▭

Part 1	Part 2	Part 3	Do not write here	Part 4
1 A B C D	8 A B C D	14	▭ 14 ▭	20 A B
2 A B C D	9 A B C D	15	▭ 15 ▭	21 A B
3 A B C D	10 A B C D	16	▭ 16 ▭	22 A B
4 A B C D	11 A B C D	17	▭ 17 ▭	23 A B
5 A B C D	12 A B C D	18	▭ 18 ▭	24 A B
6 A B C D	13 A B C D	19	▭ 19 ▭	25 A B
7 A B C D				

Picture 1

Picture 2

Picture 3

Picture 4

Key

READING

Part 1

Exercise 1 (*page 8*)

a14   b29   c24   d1   e18   f2   g4

Key phrases	indoors	outdoors	a shop	a road	a public office	public transport	a place of work	a place of entertainment
sale	✓	✓	✓					
parking		✓		✓	✓		✓	✓
no entry		✓		✓				
side door		✓				✓	✓	✓
last show	✓	✓						✓
reductions	✓	✓	✓					
passengers	✓	✓				✓		
entrance		✓		✓	✓	✓	✓	✓
exit	✓	✓	✓	✓	✓	✓	✓	✓
all breakages must be paid for	✓		✓					
staff entrance		✓	✓		✓		✓	✓
drive on left		✓		✓				
vehicle		✓		✓		✓		

Exercise 2 (*page 10*)

information	prohibition	warning	instruction
reductions	No ...ing	Warning	Please
entrance	Keep off	dangerous	Keep off
exit	Don't ...	mind ...	
open	Please don't ...	Danger	
closed	... only		
private			
... only			
... per cent off			
on sale			

Exercise 3 (*page 11*)

information   1, 4, 5, 6, 7, 8, 9, 11, 12, 13, 18, 19, 20, 21,
22, 26, 27, 28, 29, 30.
prohibition   2, 3, 5, 6, 8, 9, 11, 14, 15, 16, 17, 20, 22, 24.
warning   1, 19, 20, 22, 28.
instruction   3, 6, 10, 16, 19, 21, 23, 25, 30.

Exercise 4 (*page 11*)

a3   b20   c13, 22   d5   e8   f23

Exercise 5 (*page 12*)

1 A Incorrect.   The sign tells you 8.30 p.m. is the time the performance starts, not the length of the performance.
  B Correct.
  C Incorrect.   The performance starts at 8.30 p.m., so you should arrive **before** 8.30 p.m.
2 A Incorrect.   The sign tells you the machinery is dangerous, and not in danger of being stolen.
  B Incorrect.   The gate stops people from going into the building where the machinery is.
  C Correct.
3 A Correct.
  B Incorrect.   The sign does not tell you when the reception opens/closes.
  C Incorrect.   The reception area is open **after** 6 p.m., so people can collect their tickets.

4 A Incorrect.   The sign tells you to leave your parcel at the desk.
  B Correct.
  C Incorrect.   The sign is about delivering parcels.

TEST PRACTICE (*page 13*)

1B   2C   3D   4A   5B

Part 2

Exercise 1 (*page 14*)

	1	2	3	4	5
type of article	clothing	something for handbag	game	musical instrument	vase
for a man/woman/child	woman	woman	child	man	woman
price	less than £12				
anything else	something useful	something small	to play with friends	for a beginner	to hold flowers

Exercise 2 (*page 14*)

1 Bolivian flute.   4 mountain jumper.
2 trinket pot.   5 ring of musicians.
3 ceramic vase.

Exercise 3 (*page 14*)

1 ceramic vase.   4 Bolivian flute.
2 Ubo cards.   5 trinket pot.
3 shoulder bag.

Exercise 4 (*page 15*)

1 trinket pot   4 ring of musicians.
2 Ubo cards.   5 shoulder bag
3 ceramic vase.

Exercise 5 (*page 15*)

1 embroidered money belt.   4 Bolivian flute.
2 coin box.   5 ceramic vase.
3 Ubo cards.

Exercise 6 (*page 16*)

1 Yes, B and D.   4 Yes, C, D, E and G.
2 Yes, D.   5 No.
3 Yes, A and G.

Exercise 7 (*page 16*)

Peter
a Yes, B and D.
b Yes, A, C, E and G.
c Yes, A, B, C, D, G and H.
d Yes, A and G.
e F.

Audrey
a No.
b Yes, A, E, G and H.
c Yes, B, C, F, G and H.
d Yes, A and G.
e D.

Jenny
a No.
b Yes, A, B, D, E, F, G and H.
c Yes, D and H.
d Yes, A and G.
e C.

Gary
a Yes, B and D.
b No.
c Yes, C, D, F and H.
d Yes, A.
e E.

	Jobs							
People	A	B	C	D	E	F	G	H
1 Greg	✓	✗	✗	✗	✗	✗	✗	✗
2 Peter	✗	✗	✗	✗	✗	✓	✗	✗
3 Jenny	✗	✗	✓	✗	✗	✗	✗	✗
4 Audrey	✗	✗	✗	✓	✗	✗	✗	✗
5 Gary	✗	✗	✗	✗	✓	✗	✗	✗

TEST PRACTICE (*page 18*)

6F   7A   8G   9D   10C

Part 3

Exercise 1 (*page 20*)

1   All of the branches have a children's library.
2   The majority of branches have a reference section.
3   Most of the branches have an audio cassette library.
4   Some of the branches have photocopying.
5   Each of the branches has a children's library.
6   Every branch has a children's library.
7   Both the High Street and Belstead have a meeting room for hire.
8   A few of the branches have a video cassette library.
9   A small number of the branches have a local history section.
10 A large number of branches have a reference section.

Exercise 2 (*page 20*)

1 times   2 title   3 ages   4 cost   5 dates
6 title   7 title   8 title   9 date   10 times

Exercise 3 (*page 21*)

1A   2A   3A   4B   5B   6B   7B   8A   9B   10B

TEST PRACTICE (*page 22*)

11B   12A   13B   14A   15B
16B   17A   18A   19B   20B

Part 4

Exercise 1 (*page 23*)

1c   2a   3b

Exercise 2 (*page 24*)
2a 3b 4c 5a 6b

Exercise 3 (*page 25*)
1d 2c 3b 4e 5f 6a

Exercise 4 (*page 25*)
1C 2B 3A

TEST PRACTICE (*page 26*)
21D 22A 23D 24C 25B

Part 5

Exercise 1 (*page 28*)
1 No. It only opened three months ago.
2 Families with young children especially.
3 A children's zoo, rides on animals and a working farm.
4 They can find out what happens there and how they get their milk and eggs.
5 Because most people spend more than four hours at the zoo.

Exercise 2 (*page 28*)
2C 3D 4D 5D 6A 7C 8B 9D 10D
11C 12D 13A 14B 15A 16B 17D 18C

Exercise 3 (*page 30*)
Picture 2

Exercise 4 (*page 30*)
1B 2A 3B

Exercise 5 (*page 30*)
Passage A 1 next 2 discuss 3 in 4 meeting
5 after 6 because
Passage B 1 last 2 at 3 discussion 4 met
5 afterwards 6 so

TEST PRACTICE (*page 31*)
26B 27A 28A 29C 30B 31A 32B
33C 34C 35A

READING TEST

Part 1 (*page 32*)
1B 2A 3D 4C 5C
Part 2 (*page 33*)
6F 7A 8C 9B 10E
Part 3 (*page 34*)
11B 12A 13A 14B 15B 16B 17A
18B 19A 20A
Part 4 (*page 35*)
21A 22C 23B 24B 25C
Part 5 (*page 37*)
26D 27B 28A 29B 30A 31C 32A
33C 34D 35D

WRITING

Part 1

Exercise 1 (*page 38*)
2 There is also a small store room which can be used as an extra bedroom.
3 This block of flats was built five years ago.
4 Some have central heating during the winter months.
5 It has four floors, with four large flats on each floor.
6 New up-to-date showers were installed in all the bathrooms last year.
7 It is not possible to rent a flat for less than a week.
8 The manager's office is in the entrance hall on the ground floor.
9 The rent for flats with a sea view is higher.
10 All the flats on the upper floors can be reached by lift.

Exercise 2 (*page 39*)
2 Cups and saucers are supplied by the management.
The management supply cups and saucers.
They supply cups and saucers.
3 Laundry can be done in the basement.
You can do your laundry in the basement.
Tenants can do their laundry in the basement.
4 Cars must not be left in front of the building.
You must not leave your car in front of the building.
Tenants must not leave their cars in front of the building.
5 The full rent for your holiday flat must be paid one month in advance.
You must pay the full rent for your holiday flat one month in advance.
6 Curtains are cleaned every season.
The management clean the curtains every season.
They clean the curtains every season.
7 The manager of the flats collects rubbish daily from all the flats.
Rubbish is collected daily from all the flats [by the manager].
8 The manager can arrange dry-cleaning.
Dry-cleaning can be arranged [by the manager].
9 Dustbins can be found beside the back door.
You/One can find dustbins beside the back door.
10 The manager can order groceries for you.
Groceries can be ordered for you by the manager.
or Groceries will be delivered to your flat.
Someone will deliver groceries to your flat.

Exercise 3 (*page 40*) suggested answers

3 There is a hairdresser opposite the bus station in Fountain Square in Sandy Bay.
Sandy Bay has a hairdresser opposite the bus station in Fountain Square.

4 There are tennis courts close to the holiday flats in Sandy Bay.
Sandy Bay has some tennis courts close to the holiday flats.

5 There is a bus service to/from the bus station in Sandy Bay.
Sandy Bay has a bus service to/from the bus station.

6 There isn't a library in Sandy Bay.
Sandy Bay doesn't have a library.

7 There is a petrol station opposite the chemist in Sandy Bay.
Sandy Bay has a petrol station opposite the chemist.

8 There is a supermarket near to the chemist in Sandy Bay.
Sandy Bay has a chemist near to the supermarket.

9 There isn't a doctor in Sandy Bay.
Sandy Bay doesn't have a doctor.

10 There is a ferry to Green Island from Sandy Bay.
Sandy Bay has a ferry to Green Island.

Exercise 4 (*page 41*)

2 The Blue Moon Hotel is nearer the airport than the Seven Stars Hotel.
The Seven Stars Hotel is further from the airport than the Blue Moon Hotel.

3 The Seven Stars Hotel is older than the Blue Moon Hotel.
The Blue Moon Hotel is newer than the Seven Stars Hotel.

4 The Blue Moon Hotel has more rooms than the Seven Stars Hotel.
The Seven Stars Hotel has fewer rooms than the Blue Moon Hotel.

5 The Blue Moon Hotel is nearer Santa Rosa than the Seven Stars Hotel.
The Seven Stars Hotel is further from Santa Rosa than the Blue Moon Hotel.

7 July is warmer than June.
June is not as warm as July.

8 July is wetter than June.
June is not as wet as July.

9 August is drier than July.
July is not as dry as August.

10 August is hotter than July.
July is not as hot as August.

Exercise 5 (*page 42*) suggested answers

1 You can get onto the beach by crossing the road.
If you want to get onto the beach you should cross the road.

2 You can spend the evening dancing by going to the disco.
If you want to spend the evening dancing you can go to the disco.

3 You can hire a boat by going to the office on the beach.
If you want to hire a boat you can go to the office on the beach.

4 You can get a cold drink on the beach by buying one at the café.
If you want a cold drink on the beach, you can buy one at the café.

5 You can get to town by taking a bus.
If you want to get to town you can take a bus.

6 You can have a swim by going to the swimming pool or the beach.
If you want to have a swim you can go to the swimming pool or the beach.

7 You can hire a car by going to the garage.
If you want to hire a car you should go to the garage.

8 You can get a good suntan by going to the beach.
If you want a good suntan you should go to the beach.

9 You can catch fish by hiring a boat.
If you want to catch fish you should hire a boat.

10 You can get to Palm Island by taking the ferry.
If you want to get to Palm Island you should take the ferry.

Exercise 6 (*page 43*)

movement, correction, announcement, weight, succeed, improvement, pronunciation, attraction, practise, direction, mean, development, information, description, invade, departure, invitation, meeting, education.

Exercise 7 (*page 43*)

2 There was an advertisement for the flats in the local newspaper.
3 Their neighbours advised them.
4 The package weighs 2.5 kilograms.
5 Somebody announced the winners.
6 Their discussion of the problem lasted three hours.
7 He was educated partly in France.
8 Something new is going to develop/be developed.

TEST PRACTICE (*page 44*)

1 You can get/buy catalogues at the desk.
2 The artist did these paintings in France in 1926.
3 The Fine Arts Society held the last exhibition of the artist's work in 1966.
4 Some of the paintings in the exhibition were lent by private collectors.
5 You must leave your umbrella/all umbrellas at the desk.

Part 2

Exercise 1 (*page 45*)

2	False	5	True	8	False
3	False	6	False	9	True
4	True	7	I don't know	10	I don't know.

Exercise 2 (*page 47*) suggested answer

19th Sports and Hobbies Exhibition

VISITOR SURVEY

Date: 7 November

Personal details

Surname: Dupont   First name(s): Françoise

Nationality: French   Occupation: Office worker

Age: (tick your age group)

under 12 ☐   12 – 16 ☐   17 – 25 ✓

26 – 39 ☐   40 – 59 ☐   over 60 ☐

1 How did you hear about the exhibition?
I read about it in the newspaper.

2 What are your hobbies?
Photography and coin collecting.

3 Which stand did you find most interesting?
The photography stand.

4 What else did you like about the exhibition?
The video display.

5 Was there anything that you did not like?
The plan in the programme – it was confusing!

Exercise 3 (*page 48*)

1 J.A. Springer.
2 A bed, an armchair, a desk, a chair, a fridge, a wardrobe, a bookcase.
3 Yes, a fridge, a lamp and a stereo.
4 No.
5 No.

Exercise 4 (*page 48*)

STUDENT ACCOMMODATION SURVEY

Name .... J.A. Springer ......   Room No ...105...

Please list the furniture in the room. a bed, an armchair, a desk, a chair, a fridge, a wardrobe, a bookcase.

Please list the electrical appliances in the room. a lamp, a fridge, a stereo.

Are there any repairs that need to be done? Yes, the lamp and window are broken and the carpet has got a hole in it.

Where do you keep your food? In the fridge.

List any extra furniture you need. A wardrobe.

Signature ... J.A. Springer ...

TEST PRACTICE (*page 49*) suggested answer

STUDENT JOB CENTRE
Application for holiday work

Please supply the following information:

Surname (6) Suzuki   Initials K   [*Mr/Mrs/Miss/Ms]
*Please cross out as appropriate

Address (7) 6 Green Street Newton

Date of birth (day, month, year) (8) 5. 2. 73

PLEASE give a telephone number so that we can contact you if a job is available (9) 3432600

Type of job you want to do (10) receptionist/typist

Number of weeks you can work (11) eight

Preferred hours of work (12) 9 a.m. – 5 p.m.

Do you have any special skills? (13) Japanese and French languages ; typing

What jobs have you done before? (14) Part-time receptionist in a hotel in Tokyo for six months.

Signature (15) K. Suzuki

Part 3

Exercise 2 (*page 51*)
2 4A 3 4B 4 0p 5 3B 6 Cp 7 3A

Exercise 3 (*page 52*)
3A Then on Saturday afternoon ...
    The next thing ...
    ... in the evening.
4A ... on Sunday morning.
    The first ...
    The second ...
5A After lunch on Sunday ...
    ... first ...
    ... the last thing ...
Cp When the conference was over ... now ...

Exercise 4 (*page 53*) suggested answers

	+, – or o	a person	a place	entertainment	a sporting activity	a book	a lecture or talk	the weather
amusing	+	✓		✓		✓	✓	
disgusting	–	✓	✓	✓		✓	✓	✓
cheerful	+	✓	✓	✓			✓	
embarrassing	–	✓		✓			✓	
good-looking	+	✓						
kind	+	✓						
lovely	+	✓	✓	✓		✓	✓	✓
miserable	–	✓		✓				✓
perfect	+		✓	✓	✓	✓		✓
strange	–	✓	✓	✓	✓	✓	✓	✓
typical	o	✓	✓	✓		✓		✓

Exercise 5 (*page 53*)
Sample answer using Plan A.
Opening paragraph – no change.
    My favourite part of the conference was a discussion with some students who went to study in Britain last year. I thought that the talk about transport was very useful, too.
    Some of the other things were less interesting, I felt, such as a boring video about sightseeing in London and a confusing talk about visiting the doctor.
    We also had talks about family life, which was fairly interesting, and about history, which went on too long, although the speaker was good. It was not all talks and discussions, though. On Saturday night there was a great disco.
(Closing paragraph – no change.)

TEST PRACTICE (*page 54*)

Sample answer:
    We had a wonderful time on Saturday night. Six of us went to the Sunset Restaurant to celebrate passing our exams. It was a very special evening.
    We booked a table for eight o'clock. The food was excellent. I had spring vegetable soup, which is my favourite, followed by steak and an enormous salad. One of my friends had beef curry, but he thought it was not hot enough.
    The desserts were wonderful. I loved the chocolate ice cream. My friends had all kinds of fresh fruit, including strawberries.
    We finished the evening by dancing. The restaurant has live music on Saturday and Sunday nights. I thought the band was very good. We stayed until the restaurant closed at midnight.
    I wish you could have been with us. It was great fun.

WRITING TEST

Part 1 (*page 55*)
1 The Post Office has a complete set of telephone directories.
2 There are a lot of customers with savings accounts at the Post Office.
3 It costs more to send things by Airmail than by sea.
   or It costs less to send things by sea than by Airmail.
4 You can post valuable or urgent parcels by special service.
5 You must wrap parcels carefully and tie them with string.

Part 2 (*page 56*)

Bridge Hotel

Reservation Form

Name (6) *Roger Brown* .... *Mr/~~Mrs/Miss/Ms~~
(please delete)

Nationality (7) *English* ....

Address (8) *37 Church Street* ....
Newton ....
Derbyshire ....

Daytime Telephone No (9) *4276529* ....

Rooms required (10) *1 single room with shower*

Number of nights (11) *5*

Check in date (12) ... *2 October* ....

How will you get here? (13) *By car*

Meals required (14) *Breakfast and dinner*

Signature (15) .... *R. Brown*

Part 3 (*page 57*)
The answer should include the following.
Opening paragraph: an introduction to the subject, the weekend away, saying where you went.
In the following paragraphs you should say what you did, giving a brief description and saying whether you enjoyed the activities mentioned. Some of the settings from the photographs can be included – or you can develop your own ideas.
Closing paragraph: a concluding statement about the weekend and an informal ending to your friend.

LISTENING

Part 1

Exercise 1 (*page 58*)
Pictures:
1a with short sleeves
2a in town
3b by bus
4a at half past four
5a not open yet
6a in a hurry

Dialogues: 1a 2b 3a 4b 5b 6a

Exercise 2 (*page 59*)
1 The calendars show different dates.
2 The light bulb is missing in 3.
3 There is a cigarette in the ashtray in 3.
4 The cushion is in a different place.
5 The wastepaper basket is full in 1.
6 The teapot is missing in 3.
7 The drawer is open in 3.
8 The TV is on in 1.
9 The cassette recorder is in a different place.
10 There are two pictures on the wall in 3.
11 The time on the clock is different.

Exercise 3 (*page 59*)
The dialogue refers to picture B.

Exercise 4 (*page 60*)
The dialogue refers to picture D.

Exercise 5 (*page 60*)
The dialogue refers to picture A.

Exercise 6 (*page 60*)
dialogue 1: picture A
dialogue 2: picture C
dialogue 3: picture D

TEST PRACTICE (*page 61*)
1C 2A 3C 4B 5D 6B 7A

Part 2

Exercise 1 (*page 63*)
2 We wear ... shirts with ... sleeves. Our shirts are ...
3 We wear tracksuits ...
4 The school uniform was designed in ...

Exercise 2 (*page 63*)
1A 2A 3D 4C

Exercise 3 (*page 64*)
topics to listen for: b, r, q, m, i.

Exercise 4 *(page 64)*

1A   2B   3A   4D   5C

TEST PRACTICE *(page 65)*

8B   9D   10B   11A   12D   13C

Part 3

Exercise 1 *(page 66)*

days and dates	length of time	length (measurement)	money	weight
fourth February Monday April Sunday August first January (*Jan*) June Thursday November Wednesday (*Wed*) July third March fifth (*5th*) second (*2nd*)	minute year second (*sec*) month hour	inch feet (*ft*) yard metre centimetre (*cm*)	pound pence (*p*)	kilogram pound (*lb*) gram ounce (*oz*)

Exercise 2 *(page 67)*

2   Mon, 30/11 *or* Mon, 30 Nov.
3   85g.
4   £16.70.
5   7.00–8.15.
6   2.5m.
7   June, July, Sept.
8   90,000.
9   18 km.

Exercise 3 *(page 67)*

Weather forecast: Monday, 5 Feb
cloudy, heavy rain later
5°–7°C
light east

Date: Tues, 6 Feb	day	night
weather conditions	sunny, cloudy later	clear, frost in many places
temperature	7°–9°C	below 0°C
wind direction	strong south-west	calm
Date: Wed, 7 Feb	day	night
weather conditions	fog, sunny later	storms, very windy
temperature	6°–8°C	4°–6°C
wind direction	light west	strong north-west

TEST PRACTICE *(page 68)*

suggested answer

Name:	Annabel Green
Work:	Artist
Place of work: (14)	studio – at home
Hours of work: (15)	7.30 a.m. – 4 p.m.
Likes: (16)	working on her own
Dislikes: (17)	phone calls while working
Place of exhibition: (18)	Central Library
Dates and Times: (19)	8–14 June; 9 a.m.–5.30 p.m.

Part 4

Exercise 1 *(page 69)*

✓ = liked the speech   ✗ = disliked the speech

1 ✓   2 ✗   3 ✗   4 ✗   5 ✓   6 ✗
7 ✓   8 ✗   9 ✓   10 ✓   11 ✗   12 ✗

Exercise 2 *(page 69)*

✓ = agreement   ✗ = disagreement

1 ✓   2 ✗   3 ✓   4 ✓   5 ✗
6 ✗   7 ✗   8 ✓   9 ✗   10 ✗

Exercise 3 *(page 70)*

1   disagreeing
2   disagreeing
3   disagreeing
4   agreeing
5   agreeing
6   disagreeing
7   disagreeing
8   agreeing
9   agreeing
10   disagreeing

Exercise 4 *(page 71)*

Key phrases:
2   not happy about
3   travelling; three months a year
4   You're sure to
5   German; impressed
6   Don't you want the job?; Of course
7   German; business; French; terrible

Listening:
1B   2B   3A   4A   5A   6A   7B

TEST PRACTICE *(page 72)*

20B   21B   22A   23A   24B   25A

LISTENING TEST

Part 1 (*page 73*)
1C   2A   3B   4D   5A   6B   7C

Part 2 (*page 75*)
8A   9C   10D   11C   12A   13B

Part 3 (*page 76*)

Students' Centre

What the centre has to offer

Shop – sells food and (14) ...*newspapers*...............

Laundry – for washing and (15) ...*ironing*...............

Clinic – has a doctor, a nurse and a (16) ...*dentist*......
   Emergency number (nights only): (17) ...*7014 822*......

Advice Centre – run by (18) ...*other students*...............

Where to find the centre
New building, near the (19) ...*tower block*...............

Part 4 (*page 76*)
20A   21B   22A   23A   24B   25A

SPEAKING

Part 1

Exercise 1 (*page 77*)
1   Could you tell me your name?
2   Peter Schmidt.
3   Where are you staying?
4   At the Greenlow Hotel.
5   Could you spell that, please?
6   G-R-E-E-N-L-O-W.
7   Oh, yes. The Greenlow Hotel. Tell me, Peter, where are you from?
8   I come from Vienna.
9   Vienna? I've never been there.
10   You should go. It's an interesting place.

Exercise 3 (*page 79*)
1   right   2   wrong   3   wrong   4   right
5   right   6   wrong/right.

Exercise 5 (*page 80*)
1   Yes, thank you.
2   No, not very long. Only a few minutes.
3   It was just starting to rain.
4   Including my own language? Three altogether.
5   It's about one kilometre.
6   At the bus stop opposite the bank.

Exercise 6 (*page 81*)
2   What was that? Did you say ...?
3   Pardon? I couldn't hear that ... Did you ... or ...?
4   Could you repeat that?
5   Do you mean ...?
6   I think I understand. You ...

Part 2

Exercise 1 (*page 82*)
The students decide to go to the cinema.

Exercise 2 (*page 83*)

1d	2c	3f
4e	5a	6b

Exercise 3 (*page 83*) suggested answers
1 shall we do
2 What about going
3 we could go
4 if you prefer
5 I don't think so
6 what would you like to do
7 would really rather go
8 What a good idea

Exercise 5 (*page 84*)
A Let's go out for a meal one day this week.
B Good idea! What kind of food do you like?
A Anything really. Do you like Thai food?
B I love it. We could try that new Thai restaurant in James Street.
A Fine. Are you doing anything on Wednesday evening?
B Yes, I have to work late. The end of the week's probably better for me.
A Are you free on Friday?
B Yes, I think so. It'll be busy so we'd better book. What time shall we go?
A 8 o'clock?
B Can we make it 8.30?
A Sure. I'll call and book now.

Exercise 6 (*page 84*) suggested answer)
A What kind of video would you like to get?
B How/What about a good horror film?
A No, I don't think so. I'd rather see something a bit lighter.
B Well, we could get a comedy if you like. It would be good to see something really funny. Go on, we haven't seen one for ages.
A OK. What about something like *Planes, Trains and Automobiles*?
B It's great, but I've seen it so many times. Have you ever seen *Throw Momma from the Train*? It's hilarious.
A No, let's get that one.
B Are you doing anything on Monday evening?
A I'm afraid so. I've got to work late.
B What about Tuesday at about 7 o'clock?
A Yes, that would be fine.

Part 3

Exercise 1 (*page 86*) suggested answer

Table 1: Background	definitely	probably
place	a station	
town or country		country or a small town
season	not winter	summer, autumn
weather	fine and sunny	fairly cool
time of day	daytime	

Table 2: People	definitely	probably
how many		15–20
ages	all	
occupations	some tourists	1 engine driver
clothes	holiday clothes	driver–work clothes
mood	relaxed	

Table 3: Action	definitely	probably
moving	taking photos	waiting for the train to leave
preparing to		drive the train get on the train
holding	cameras bags a baby	

Exercise 6 (*page 89*)

1   The woman in 4 is not wearing a watch.
2   The window is open in 4.
3   The woman is standing in 4, sitting in 2.
4   The child is reading a book in 2, a comic in 4.
5   The man is holding a knife in 4, a spoon in 2.
6   There are four mugs in 2, three in 4.
7   There are three chairs in 2, four in 4.
8   There are oranges in the bowl in 2, apples in 4.
9   The man is not wearing a tie in 2.
10   The time is different.

Part 4

Exercise 1 (*page 91*)

a2   b3   c3   d1   e2   f2   g1

Exercise 2 (*page 91*)

1a   2d   3g   4b   5f   6c   7e

Practice test key

READING

Part 1 (*page 95*)

1B 2B 3A 4C 5A

Part 2 (*page 96*)

6G 7D 8C 9E 10A

Part 3 (*page 97*)

11B 12A 13B 14A 15B 16B 17B
18A 19A 20A

Part 4 (*page 98*)

21C 22A 23B 24D 25C

Part 5 (*page 99*)

26B 27D 28C 29B 30A 31B 32B
33D 34A 35C

WRITING

Part 1 (*page 100*)

1 There is a new library at the college with plenty of room to study.
   There is plenty of room to study in the college's new library.
2 The science department offers six different courses.
3 Students from abroad like the computer courses very much.
4 The ordinary business course does not last as long as the advanced business course.
   The ordinary business course is shorter than the advanced business course.
5 If students are successful, they will receive a certificate.

Part 2 (*page 101*)

SPORTS WEEKEND APPLICATION FORM

Name (6) .. *Mary Preston* ....   *Mr/Mrs/Miss/Ms
                                         (*please delete)

Address (7) .. *17 Red House Lane* ......
.... *Trentford* ....
.... *Leicestershire* ....
....

Tel No .. *0582 13689* ....
Nationality (8) .. *English* ....
Date of birth (day, month, year) (9) ... *3. 9. 77*

Where do you usually play sports? (10) ... *At Trentford*
.... *High School* ....
....

Which sport would you like to join in? (11) ... *Swimming* .
....
....

What sports equipment do you need to borrow? (12) ....
.... *None* ....
....

What is your best sport? How long have you been playing?
(13) .. *Tennis – five years (now in the* ......
.... *school team)* ....

Could you help to organize a sport? Which sport could you
help with? (14) .. *Yes , tennis* ......
....

Signature (15) ... *M. Preston* ....

Part 3 (*page 102*)
Your answer should include the following:
Opening paragraph: greet Jim Mitchell, introduce yourself
and explain why you are writing.
In the following paragraphs you should give the
information asked for in the question – your age, interests,
the kind of work you are interested in and the reasons
why.
Closing paragraph: conclude your letter (hoping to hear
from Jim Mitchell soon).

LISTENING

Part 1 (*page 103*)
1C   2A   3D   4A   5B   6D   7C

Part 2 (*page 105*)
8C   9A   10C   11D   12C   13C

Part 3 (*page 106*)
14   the basement.
15   kettles and irons.
16   diet menu.
17   suitcases.
18   the music department.
19   ten per cent.

Part 4 (*page 106*)
20A   21B   22A   23B   24A   25A

Tapescript

—— WRITING ——

Part 1

Exercise 3 (page 40)

Booking clerk Hello, can I help you?

Mrs Taylor Well, yes. We're thinking of renting one of your flats at Sandy Bay. Could you give me some information about the area?

Booking clerk Yes, of course. We'll send you a map of Sandy Bay. But would you like me to tell you anything right now?

Mrs Taylor Well, just a few details, if you don't mind. First of all, is there a beach?

Booking clerk Yes, the flats have their own beach at the bottom of the cliffs. There are some steps leading down to the beach from the flats.

Mrs Taylor Thanks. And is there a golf course nearby?

Booking clerk Yes, indeed there is. Sandy Bay has a very good golf course, right across the bay from the flats.

Mrs Taylor Thanks. That's good to know.

Booking clerk If you give me your address, I'll send you an information leaflet about the flats and a map of the area.

Mrs Taylor Thank you very much. My name's Mrs Taylor and . . .

—— LISTENING ——

Part 1

Exercise 1 (page 58)

1 **A** Can I help you?
   B Yes, I'd like to try on a shirt. Not too dear. And with short sleeves, if possible.

2 **A** Now, tell me about your new house. Where is it?
   B It's not very big. It's in the country.

3 **A** Hello, you're early. How did you get here? By car?
   B No, I came by train this time.

4 **A** Thank you so much for asking us. What time shall we come?
   B Why don't you come round at a quarter past four?

5 **A** Before we go back, I've got to go to the greengrocer. I need some carrots for supper.
   B Isn't it too late?
   A No, they're still open.

6 **A** Have you spoken to Tina about the school sports?
   B Not yet. I saw her yesterday, but she was in a hurry.

Exercise 6 (page 60)

1 **A** Excuse me. Is there anywhere around here where I can park my car?
   B Er . . . yes. Turn left at the crossroads, then turn right just after the zebra crossing. The car park's at the back of the clinic.

2 **A** Did you manage to get everything on my list?
   B I think so. Let's see . . . two bottles of milk, half a dozen eggs, a bottle of lemonade, two loaves of bread, two packets of biscuits and half a pound of flour. I don't think I've forgotten anything.

3 **A** How will I recognize Mr Sullivan when I meet him?
   B Well, he's not very tall, with broad shoulders. He's got a thin moustache, and dark curly hair. He'll have a dark blue jacket and grey trousers on, and he'll be carrying a light-coloured case.

TEST PRACTICE

Part 1 (page 61)

There are seven questions in this Part. For each question there are four pictures and a short recording. You will hear each recording twice. For each question, look at the pictures and listen to the recording. Choose the correct picture and put a tick in the box below it. Before we start, here is an example.

A Excuse me. Could you tell me the way to the police station, please?

B Yes . . . let me see . . . turn left at the crossroads and take the second turning on the right. The police station is just on the left – you can't miss it.

(Pause . . . Repeat . . . Pause)

The man is asking where the police station is. So the first picture is the most suitable and the tick has been put in the box under that picture.

Now we are ready to start. Here is a short recording for the first four pictures. Don't forget to put a tick in one of the boxes. Listen carefully.

1 **A** See that shop? That's where I bought my new computer.
   B Oh, yes. It's next to the shop where I bought my trainers.

(Pause . . . Repeat . . . Pause)

2 **A** Is this yours?
   B Is it blue with a brown handle?
   A Let me take a look. Yes, it is.
   B Then it must be mine. Thank you.

(Pause . . . Repeat . . . Pause)

3 **A** Do I look all right?
   B Well, yes. You look fine, except that your socks don't match.
(Pause . . . Repeat . . . Pause)

4 **A** Which earrings do you prefer?
   B I think I like the long blue and white ones.
(Pause . . . Repeat . . . Pause)

5 **A** Have you ordered your lunch?
   B Yes, I'm having sausages, egg and chips.
   A Anything to drink?
   B Just a glass of milk.
(Pause . . . Repeat . . . Pause)

6 **A** Are these the photos you took on holiday?
   B Yes. Look at this one. Here I am with my wife and the two children. The weather wasn't so good that day, unfortunately. You can see our hotel in the background.
(Pause . . . Repeat . . . Pause)

7 **A** You look tired.
   B Yes, I've been working hard. There were a lot of patients in the waiting room. One of them had two small children with her. It was all very noisy, and I've got a headache now.
(Pause . . . Repeat . . . Pause)

That is the end of Part 1. You now have half a minute to check your answers.

Part 2

Exercise 2 *(page 63)*

Interviewer   There has been a lot of argument recently about school uniforms. Some people like them, others don't. Well today Sharon, a fourth form pupil at Castleton High School, is going to talk about her school uniform.
    First of all, Sharon, could you describe your school uniform to the listeners?

Sharon   Yes, well, our school colours are blue and grey. The girls wear grey skirts and the boys, of course, wear grey trousers. We all wear blue shirts with long sleeves, and grey jackets or sweaters.
    We wear this uniform all the time, from Monday to Friday, except for when we have games. We wear tracksuits for games.
    The uniform is quite traditional really. I believe it used to be different. I've got some pictures of my aunt when she was at school, and they wore a different uniform then. It was changed in the sixties. This uniform was designed in 1966. It's quite old-fashioned, now, really.

Exercise 4 *(page 64)*

Here is the Entertainment Guide for this week. It's going to be an exciting week, too. All kinds of things are going on. Following last year's very successful exhibition in the Town Hall, there is another exhibition of posters. Last year it was early holiday posters; this year is rather similar, but this time the exhibition will be of railway posters. The exhibition opened on Monday and will be in the Town Hall until the end of next week. Admission is free, and the exhibition is open from ten until five every day.

There's a special feature at the Arts Centre this week. It's the very first performance of a new play, *The Rose Garden*, by a local writer, Alan Brown. This is Alan's first stage play, but many of you have enjoyed his films on television. The play will be on every evening this week. It finishes on Saturday, so be sure to book your seats, if you have not done so already.

You can book seats for *The Rose Garden*, and for the film, *Detective in the Shadows*, which is being shown this week at the Arts Centre cinema. The place to go to make reservations is the Tourist Centre, which also has details of many other things that are going on this summer.

The Tourist Centre is open from nine-thirty until four-thirty every day except Sunday and Monday.

Looking forward to next month, a lot of people, especially children, will be delighted to hear that the circus is making a return visit towards the end of the month. Next week, I hope I can give you more details of this . . .

TEST PRACTICE

Part 2 *(page 65)*

Look at the questions for Part 2. You will hear a recording of a teacher talking about a school trip. Put a tick in the correct box for each question. At the end, the recording is repeated.
(Pause) *Now we are ready to start. Listen carefully.*

Right, everyone, thanks for coming. I hope this won't take too long. As it's only a week until the school trip, I'm going to tell you what you need to bring with you. Listen carefully – you mustn't leave any essential things behind. Now, we're going for two days, not two weeks, so you should take only a small bag, with the right clothes and no extras. We're going to be outside for much of the time, so pack some warm clothes for day time, including jeans or trousers and a thick sweater. Make sure you have a pair of strong sensible shoes for walking. Oh and don't forget to pack some spare socks, just in case your feet get wet. You needn't bring a towel unless you plan to go swimming – and of course, if you do, don't forget your swimming costume. For the evening, you should have some different clothes. We've organized something special for you.

There'll be a meal for the whole group, followed by dancing at the disco. So you need suitable clothes for that. You don't need to be dressed in the latest fashion, just what you feel comfortable in. Well, that's it, I think. But seriously, don't bring too much, okay? You'll have to carry your own luggage, remember. (FADE OUT)

(Pause) *Now listen again.*

(Repeat recording.)

That is the end of Part 2.

You now have a minute to check your answers.

Part 3

Exercise 2 (*page 67*)

1 It's half past two. Your watch is fifteen minutes slow.
2 The postcard was dated Monday, November 30th.
3 The contents of this envelope weigh eighty-five grams.
4 The return fare is sixteen pounds seventy pence.
5 Breakfast will be served from seven o'clock until a quarter past eight.
6 The width of the material is two point five metres.
7 The experiments will carry on in June, July and September.
8 The population fell to less than ninety thousand last year.
9 From my home to the city centre is a distance of eighteen kilometres.

Exercise 3 (*page 67*)

Here is the weather forecast for the next three days. First, the forecast for tomorrow, Monday the fifth of February.

It will be cloudy at first during the day, but later on the weather will become worse and there will be heavy rain. The temperature during the day will be between five and seven degrees celsius. At night temperatures will drop to between zero and two degrees celsius and the showers of rain will turn into snow. Throughout the day the wind will be light, blowing from the south-east. At night, the wind will come from the east.

Here is the forecast for Tuesday the sixth of February. It will be warmer at first, with daytime temperatures rising to between seven and maybe nine degrees celsius. At first the sun will shine, and most of the snow will disappear altogether. Later on in the afternoon the wind from the south-west will become stronger and it will bring clouds with it. The clouds will disappear by nightfall and the wind will drop. It will be a calm, clear night with frost in many places. Night-time temperatures will fall below zero celsius.

And this is the forecast for Wednesday the seventh of February. In the morning it will be foggy at first, but the fog will disappear before noon. Then the sun will shine for a time, and there will be light winds from the west. By the end of the day the wind will have changed direction and will bring stormy weather from the north-west. The storms will continue throughout the night with very strong winds. The temperature will be between six and eight degrees celsius during the day, falling to between four and six degrees celsius at night.

TEST PRACTICE

Part 3 (*page 68*)

Look at the notes about Annabel Green. Some information is missing. You will hear Annabel talking about herself. For each question, fill in the missing information in the numbered space. You will hear the recording twice.

Now we are ready to start. Listen carefully.

Interviewer Continuing our series about people at work, I went out last week to talk to a young artist, Annabel Green. (FADE OUT)

Annabel As an artist, I work completely on my own. I work here, in my small studio at home. It's very peaceful in the country. I never feel lonely when I'm working – I have my two cats to keep me company. I always start work quite early in the morning, almost as soon as I'm up – no later than half past seven. Then I work right through the day. I finish most days around four. Sometimes I work later, but usually, it's about four when I finish – especially in the winter, when it gets dark so early.

I really like working on my own. It's nice to be able to listen to music while I'm working. It's good to have loud music to work to! The thing I really hate is when the telephone rings. It stops me working. People do need to phone me, and of course, I want to get orders for pictures – but it is very annoying to get a phone call right in the middle of everything.

There's going to be a public exhibition of my work at the Central Library. It's my first exhibition. It will be on from the eighth to the fourteenth of June. It's free and it will be open from nine in the morning until half past five. I'm looking forward to it very much.

(Pause) *Now listen again.*

(Repeat recording.)

That is the end of Part 3.

You now have a minute to check your answers.

Part 4

Exercise 1 (*page 69*)

1 I admire the speaker. She began at once with the question of cost, which is after all what we are all anxious about. She did a good job.

2 Well, she wasn't such a bad speaker, I suppose. But at the same time, she didn't manage to persuade me to agree with her.

3 She seemed to be afraid of saying what she really believed in. She didn't defend the people whose lives will be nearly destroyed by the motorway.

4 These speakers are all alike. They make me feel depressed. I can't tell one from another. I was bored, to be frank.

5 This is one of the most honest speeches I've heard so far. It was a change from the usual arguments we've been hearing recently.

6 It was a rather weak speech, I thought. I was astonished that she didn't make it clear whose fault it was that those crazy plans were accepted in the first place.

7 Anyway, she was very brave to attack by name certain government officers. We all know now who is to blame for all the mistakes that have been made in the past. We need people like her to represent us.

8 The audience was very patient. I could hardly keep awake, and a man in the row behind ours actually fell asleep. The speech was very badly written.

9 I thought it was an intelligent speech. Some people thought it was a bit long, but personally I didn't mind that.

10 She really seemed to care about the results of this project. She has certainly influenced my thinking. I feel like joining in a demonstration against the motorway.

11 Well, the audience clapped a lot. But, in the end, there was nothing of extraordinary importance in the speech. Very disappointing, I felt.

12 It was all, well, a bit too serious. There were no jokes; the audience never laughed. A good speaker usually says something funny. Yet it wasn't really what you'd call a powerful speech either, was it?

Exercise 3 (*page 70*)

1 **A** Are you sure you want to go to the meeting tonight?
B Yes, I am, and I think you should go too.
A Well, surely we don't both need to go.

2 **A** I'm going to wear my new lipstick for the interview.
B Are you really? Don't you think it's a bit bright?

3 **A** Do you think I should apply to join the police force?
B Well . . . not really. I don't think you have the right qualifications.

A Well, I think I'd make a good policeman.

4 **A** Wouldn't you like to go somewhere hot for your holiday?
B That's a wonderful idea.

5 **A** You're absolutely right. This sweater is too long.
B I'm glad you think so. Try this one on instead.

6 **A** To get to Joe's house, we need to take the first turning on the left.
B Are you quite certain about that? I thought it was in the opposite direction.

7 **A** Let's go to that nice restaurant. You know, the one we went to last time we were here.
B That one? I can't believe you thought it was nice. I think we should try somewhere else.

8 **A** What a pity! The film we wanted to see isn't on this week.
B Yes, I'm afraid we're unlucky again.

9 **A** Steve is late again. I'm sure he does it on purpose!
B I see what you mean. He always seems to be the last to arrive.

10 **A** Gemma's certain to pass her exam.
B I doubt it. She only started to revise for it last week.

Exercise 4 (*page 71*)

Woman Aren't you going for that job interview tomorrow?
Man That's right. I have to go at ten o'clock in the morning. I don't know how to get there, though.
Woman I can take you there in my car, if you like.
Man Thanks a lot. That's a great help. I must say, I'm not happy about this interview.
Woman Why not? You've got the right qualifications. And I know they need engineers.
Man I know, but I haven't had much experience.
Woman I don't think that matters. You're sure to get the job.
Man I don't know. I don't feel very confident about it.
Woman Don't you want the job?
Man Of course I do. I really need it.
Woman Will it involve a lot of travelling?
Man About three months a year, they said in the advertisement. And that's another thing. I don't think I'm good enough at languages.
Woman But your German is really fluent. I was very impressed by the way you talked to those people we met on holiday last year.
Man But I don't think I speak German well enough for doing business, and my French is terrible.
Woman Well, I don't agree, your languages are good.
Man It's very nice of you to try to cheer me up, but I still don't think I'm going to get the job.
Woman Well, we'll just have to wait and see, won't we?

TEST PRACTICE

Part 4 *(page 72)*

Look at the six statements for this Part. You will hear a conversation between a woman and a man. Decide if you think each statement is correct or incorrect. If you think it is correct, put a tick in the box under A. If you think it is not correct, put a tick in the box under B. At the end the recording is repeated.

(Pause) Now we are ready to start. Listen carefully.

Woman	What are you wearing for the party tomorrow night?
Man	Well, I thought I'd wear my jeans.
Woman	What! For a party! You can't do that.
Man	Why not? I wear a suit for work every day. I'm tired of wearing suits. I want to wear something different when I go out. I want to feel comfortable.
Woman	But you can't wear your jeans.
Man	I don't see why not. They're not dirty.
Woman	Well, they're not very smart, are they? They're not the latest fashion. And I'm wearing a party dress.
Man	Which dress?
Woman	The red one. Why? Don't you like it?
Man	Well, yes . . . I like it. But it's not really suitable for tomorrow night. It won't be that kind of party.
Woman	What kind of party will it be, then?
Man	Well, just a few old friends getting together.
Woman	Are you sure? I heard there would be a lot of people there.
Man	Who told you that?
Woman	Sarah.
Man	Oh. Well, in that case, perhaps I won't wear my jeans.
Woman	Good. And should I wear my red dress?
Man	Well, yes, I think you should.

(Pause) Now listen again.

(Repeat recording.)

That is the end of Part 4. You now have twelve minutes to check and transfer your answers to the Answer Sheet.

——— LISTENING TEST ———

Preliminary English Test. There are four Parts to the Test. You will hear each recording twice. During the Test there will be a pause before each Part to allow you to look through the questions, and other pauses to let you think about your answers. You should write your answers on the Question Paper. You will have twelve minutes at the end to transfer your answers to the separate Answer Sheet.

Part 1 *(page 73)*

There are seven questions in this Part. For each question there are four pictures and a short recording. You will hear each recording twice. For each question, look at the pictures and listen to the recording. Choose the correct picture and put a tick in the box below it.

Before we start, here is an example:

A   There must be a mistake here!
B   What's the matter?
A   It's the electricity company. They've sent me a bill for a hundred and fifteen pounds, but I'm sure it shouldn't be that much!

(Pause . . . Repeat . . . Pause)

The woman says that she has received a bill for a hundred and fifteen pounds, so the second picture is the most suitable and the tick has been put in the box under that picture.

Now we are ready to start. Here is a short recording for the first four pictures. Don't forget to put a tick in one of the boxes. Listen carefully.

1   **A**   Would you pass the pepper please?
    B   What was that?
    A   The pepper. It's between the toast and the jam jar.
(Pause . . . Repeat . . . Pause)

2   **A**   Come on, we'll have to get out of here now if we want to get back on time!
    B   All right, but I've got to comb my hair first.
(Pause . . . Repeat . . . Pause)

3   **A**   Oh dear! The head teacher's been in this classroom.
    B   How do you know?
    A   Look! That's her handwriting on the blackboard, in white chalk.
(Pause . . . Repeat . . . Pause)

4   **A**   Look out as you approach the traffic lights!
    B   What's the matter?
    A   There's a van which has broken down.
(Pause . . . Repeat . . . Pause)

5   **A**   Did you say your nephew was in here?
    B   Yes, there he is, playing cards with those boys over there, beside the piano. He's the one sitting down with his jacket off.
(Pause . . . Repeat . . . Pause)

6   **A**   Have you laid the table yet?
    B   Well, it's partly laid. I've put my books away and laid the table cloth and the knives and forks, but I haven't found the plates or the cups and saucers yet.
(Pause . . . Repeat . . . Pause)

7   **A**   You'll find Gill in the garden.
    B   Oh? What's she doing? Picking flowers?
    A   No . . . I don't think so. She's taken my spade so I think she must be digging a hole to plant the new rose bush.
(Pause . . . Repeat . . . Pause)

That is the end of Part 1. You now have half a minute to check your answers. We will tell you when Part 2 begins.

Part 2 (*page 75*)

Now turn to Part 2, questions 8 to 13. Look at the questions for this Part. You will hear a recording of a radio report of traffic conditions. Put a tick in the correct box for each question. At the end the recording is repeated.

(Pause) *Now we are ready to start. Listen carefully.*

Hello. Here is the report of local traffic conditions for Tuesday the eleventh of February.

There is ice on roads everywhere in the north-west, which is causing delays on the route to the airport. The ice will melt later in the morning, but a further drop in temperature is expected in the late afternoon.

In the river valley, fog, which is thick in places, is making it dangerous to overtake, the police warn. They strongly advise drivers of motor vehicles to go more carefully.

We have received news of a bad accident on the valley road, where it joins the main Highfield road. Ambulances have been sent to the scene, but no deaths have been reported.

The traffic is behaving normally on the eastern routes into the city centre, except on the steep hill between Kingsgate Police Station and Wood Lane, where a lorry has hit a tree and lost its load. There is a speed limit of twenty miles per hour in this area. Drivers are advised to turn back if possible and use the road through Forest Hill. It is probable that the road will be cleared in two hours.

Travellers to the continent will find the hovercraft service operating as usual. Weather conditions at sea are rough, with strong winds and high waves. The hovercraft operators report that the service is crowded for a weekday, and advise travellers to arrive early to be sure to get a place on board.

We have been informed that traffic may be held up on the principal roads to the coast because the repairs to the harbour bridge, which carries traffic to the hovercraft port, are still only half finished.

Finally a word of warning to those of you who are out for a walk or riding your bike as it grows dark. Please wear bright colours so that you can be seen. There have recently been cases of people being run down on country roads.

Well, that's all for now. Goodbye! And if you are on a journey – take care!

(Pause) *Now listen again.*

(Repeat recording.)

That is the end of Part 2. You now have a minute to check your answers. We will tell you when Part 3 begins.

Part 3 (*page 76*)

Now turn to Part 3, questions 14 to 19. Look at the notes about the students' centre. Some information is missing. You will hear a student talking about the centre. For each question, fill in the missing information in the numbered space. You will hear the recording twice.

Now we are ready to start. Listen carefully.

We use the students' centre a lot. The college is quite a long way from the middle of town, on the top of a hill. Having the centre means for example that we don't have to travel into town every time we want to do some shopping. The shop has essential food – things like milk, bread, eggs, tins of food – and it also sells newspapers. It's a really useful place! Then there's the laundry, with six new washing machines – and we can do ironing there, too. Not that I do much of that, I must say. More importantly, there's a clinic which employs a full-time doctor and a nurse, and even a dentist. That's only during the day, of course. If a student has a problem at night there's an emergency phone number – 701 4822 – where you are always put through to a doctor. So we're very well looked after! Another important thing is the advice centre, which is open 24 hours a day. Students like to be independent, but if they need someone's help, they can come in to the advice centre and talk things through. Whatever their problems, students need to talk to people they can trust, so having other students in charge of the advice centre works really well. What's nice about the centre is that it's a new building – and an unusual one at that. It's oval in shape and has a lot of glass, which makes it feel a bright and happy place to be in. And it's very convenient too, as it's so close to the tower block where most students live. The centre's brilliant! I don't think we could manage without it.

(Pause) *Now listen again.*

(Repeat recording)

That is the end of Part 3. You now have a minute to check your answers. We will tell you when Part 4 begins.

Part 4 (*page 76*)

*Now turn to Part 4, questions 20 to 25. Look at the six statements for this Part. You will hear a conversation between a woman and a man. Decide if you think each statement is correct or incorrect. If you think it is correct, put a tick in the box under **A**. If you think it is not correct, put a tick in the box under **B**. At the end the recording is repeated.*

(Pause) *Now we are ready to start. Listen carefully.*

Woman You're going on holiday soon, aren't you?

Man Yes, next month, but to tell you the truth, I'm not feeling very happy about it. I'm a bit worried about my health.

Woman Really? What a shame! You do look a bit pale. What's the matter with you?

Man Oh, nothing's wrong with me now. But there may be insects out there that sting and bite. I've got this fear of being bitten by insects and catching some disease. I hear there's a lot of dirt and disease in hot countries.

Woman Nonsense. Just take some cream for the insect bites.

Man Yes, I will. I'm taking a lot of pills, too. I've got some pills to help me to sleep on the plane, then some pills to kill the pain if I get stomach-ache, or a headache or earache. But I'm afraid the heat might make me feel faint.

Woman I'm sure it won't. There'll be fans or air conditioning in your hotel to cool the air. Anyhow, it won't be very hot at this time of year. If you keep in the shade and make sure your skin doesn't burn, you'll be all right. You know, it's stupid to let these worries spoil your holiday.

Man Well, I don't know . . .

Woman Believe me. I went to the same place last year. I had a wonderful time. When I got back I felt great. I'd never felt so well. I had a wonderful rest, and got a great tan too.

Man Now I feel ashamed for feeling so nervous about it. So you truly think I've got nothing to worry about?

Woman Nothing at all. You should just go ahead and enjoy your holiday.

(Pause) *Now listen again.*

(Repeat recording.)

That is the end of Part 4. You now have twelve minutes to check and transfer your answers to the Answer Sheet.

——— SPEAKING ———

Part 1

Exercise 3 (*page 79*)

1 **A** Just remind me. How do you spell the name of the restaurant?
   B C-O-R-N-U-C-O-P-I-A.
   A Thanks.

2 **A** Do you know the phone number of that dry cleaning place in Hastings?
   B Yes, here it is. Have you got a pencil?
   A Yes.
   B It's nine oh seven double one.

3 **A** How do you spell the sales manager's surname?
   B K...
   A Just a moment. I'll write it down. Okay. Go ahead.
   B K-O-double S-O-F-S-K-Y.

4 **A** What's the name of that garage in Sylvester Square?
   B Rivermead.
   A How do you spell it?
   B R-I-V-E-R-M-E-A-D.
   A Thanks.

5 **A** Does the garage have a telephone number for emergencies?
   B Yes it does. It's double one four seven five oh.

6 **A** Could you help me? I'm trying to find the number of the Excaliber Oil Company.
   B Would you mind spelling the name of the Company, please?
   A It's E-X-C-A-L-I-B-E-R.
   B Thanks. The number is oh five four oh, double six, double two, double nine.

Exercise 5 (*page 80*)

1 Are you ready to start the interview?
2 Well. Have you been waiting long?
3 I hope you didn't get wet. When you came in, what was the weather like?
4 There's no need to be nervous. Tell me, how many languages can you speak?
5 How far is it to your house from here?
6 And when you leave here, where will you catch the bus?

Exercise 6 *(page 81)*

Student I must apologize for being late. My car ...
Woman I'm sorry, I didn't hear that.
Student Yes. I'm late because my car ...
Woman What was that? Did you say something happened to your car?
Student Yes, it broke down.
Woman Oh, I see. Poor you.
Student So I had to ...
Woman Pardon? I couldn't hear that. Did you catch a bus or a train?
Student Neither. I had to ...
Woman Could you repeat that?
Student I had to get a lift from ...
Woman Oh. Do you mean you got a lift from your father?
Student No, ... a neighbour of mine.
Woman Oh. I think I understand. You had to get a lift from your neighbour.
Student Yes.

Part 2

Exercise 1 *(page 82)*

A What shall we do this evening?
B What about going to see *Hamlet*? I've heard it's really good.
A Oh, I don't know. The last time I went to see a Shakespeare play, I fell asleep.
B Really? This production is set in this century, and they say it's quite unusual. I suppose we could go to the disco or a restaurant if you prefer.
A I don't think so. Certainly not the disco, anyway. The music was awful last time we went.
B Well, what would you like to do?
A I think the others in the class would really rather go to see the film at the Odeon – it's that new thriller that everyone's talking about. What do you think? Would you like to go?
B Oh yes. What a good idea! Let's see what the others think.

Part 4

Exercise 2 *(page 91)*

1   No, not really. I only started to learn last year. There wasn't a pool in the place where I used to live.
2   No, but I've always wanted to have a dog or a cat. Unfortunately, we live in an apartment which is too small.
3   Yes, I am. My uncle used to own a farm. I used to go there when I was little and help to feed the cows and pigs. There was a lovely old horse there, too, and I used to ride it round a field. It couldn't go very fast, but I was very excited. The horse seemed to be enormous.
4   Not very often. I hate crowds, and I always seem to have other things to do at the weekends. Sometimes I go with my mother, but usually I try to avoid it. I know some people love looking around shops, but I think it's very boring and tiring.
5   I don't really, I'm afraid. I know everybody should take some exercise, but my school work seems to keep me busy most of the time. I don't think I'm especially unhealthy, though. Actually, I've been thinking of taking up cycling again. I used to enjoy it a lot when I was younger.
6   It's hard to say, I seem to like everything, but I think cheese is my favourite. I usually have some for lunch with an apple or a piece of celery. When I go out for a meal I like to have a very hot curry, with lots of rice.
7   No, I'm not. I've never had the chance to do any. My cousin took me out in a boat once when I was very young, and I hated it. I think I was frightened. I like some other kinds of sports, though, especially football.

—— PRACTICE TEST PAPER ——

Preliminary English Test. There are four Parts to the Test. You will hear each recording twice. During the Test there will be a pause before each Part to allow you to look through the questions, and other pauses to let you think about your answers. You should write your answers on the Question Paper. You will have twelve minutes at the end to transfer your answers to the separate Answer Sheet.

Part 1 *(page 103)*

There are seven questions in this Part. For each question there are four pictures and a short recording. You will hear each recording twice. For each question, look at the pictures and listen to the recording. Choose the correct picture and put a tick in the box below it.

Before we start, here is an example:
A Is the place where you are staying near the airport?
B No, it's quite a long way from it, actually.
A So how will you get from the airport to your hotel?
B Well, it's too far to take a taxi, so we've decided to hire a car and drive there.
(Pause ... Repeat ... Pause)

The man says that they are going to hire a car, so the third picture is the most suitable and the tick has been put in the box under that picture.

Now we are ready to start. Here is a short recording for the first four pictures. Don't forget to put a tick in one of the boxes. Listen carefully.

1 **A** I like that sweater.
  B Which sweater?
  A That one. The green one with white spots.
(Pause ... Repeat ... Pause)

2 **A** Excuse me. I'm looking for the manager's office.
  B The manager's office? It's the door facing you at the top of the stairs.
  A Thanks.
(Pause ... Repeat ... Pause)

3 **A** Could you get me my book, please?
  B Yes of course. Where is it?
  A It's on the table beside my bed, the one with the lamp.
(Pause ... Repeat ... Pause)

4 **A** What do you want for lunch?
  B Nothing much. I'm in a hurry.
  A Well, how about a cup of coffee and a sandwich?
  B That sounds fine.
(Pause ... Repeat ... Pause)

5 **A** How are you getting on?
  B I've nearly finished. I've typed the letter, but I haven't done the envelope yet.
(Pause ... Repeat ... Pause)

6 **A** Has Harry told you about his plans?
  B Yes, he has, as it happens. He says he's catching the train at eleven.
  A Is he travelling on his own?
  B No. He's got his niece with him. She's only six.
(Pause ... Repeat ... Pause)

7 **A** Did you find the house?
  B Yes, I did, in the end. It was at the end of a long lane.
  A Was it near the village?
  B No. There wasn't another house in sight. There was a small wood behind it, and fields on either side.
(Pause ... Repeat ... Pause)

That is the end of Part 1. You now have half a minute to check your answers. We will tell you when Part 2 begins.

Part 2 *(page 105)*

Now turn to Part 2, questions 8 to 13. Look at the questions for this Part. You will hear a recording of a radio report about summer courses at a school. Put a tick in the correct box for each question. At the end the recording is repeated.

(Pause) Now we are ready to start. Listen carefully.

This is Radio Benfield. Now, some information on schools and colleges in the Benfield area. First I am going to tell you about the Benfield School of English, which is run by Mrs Sylvia Spring. This year, the school is offering new summer courses, which sound very good indeed. Mrs Spring and her team have made a lot of changes since last year and they are able to offer many more conversation classes than before. There will be at least three hours a day, five days a week. And for about half of these classes the students will be working in groups of seven or eight.

Courses on reading and writing will also be given. There's a completely new reading course, in fact, which Mrs Spring believes the students will find very interesting. Teachers will use current newspaper articles and other material. For the first time this year, the school is running a computer course, too. The school will also be continuing the video course, which was very popular last year. Benfield School has some new video equipment and the teachers know a lot about video.

All this sounds like hard work! But there will be a lot of leisure activities too. Mrs Spring has arranged for students to use the sports centre near the school in the afternoons and evenings, at greatly reduced prices. And the school has planned a lot of visits to places of interest in the neighbourhood. There will be some special surprises for the students, as well. Mrs Spring has organized a group visit to a television studio, as a suitable end to the video course. I'm sure everyone will find that really exciting.

Mrs Spring is also hoping that some students will be able to take flying lessons at the airport, which will again be a first for Benfield School of English.

The school only takes between forty and fifty students at a time, which means that it provides classes and activities where students can feel they are among friends. Although it is a small school, only a few of the students stay at the school itself, in one of two flats in the main building. Most of the summer students will stay with families in the town.

So, that's Benfield School of English – an excellent school, with a lot to offer. Next, we look at an art college that has just ... (FADE)

(Pause) Now listen again.

(Repeat recording.)

That is the end of Part 2. You now have a minute to check your answers. We will tell you when Part 3 begins.

Part 3 (page 106)

Now turn to Part 3 questions 14 to 19. You will hear a recording of an announcement in a department store. For each question, fill in the missing information in the numbered space. At the end, the recording is repeated.

(Pause) *Now we are ready to start. Listen carefully.*

Welcome to Walton's department store. This month we have some exciting new offers for you.

First of all, there is a sale of quality electrical equipment, including coffee makers, kettles and irons. You will find these in the basement.

Also for the whole of this month, there will be a special diet menu, including fresh salads in the café on the third floor. And while you are on the third floor, don't miss our fine exhibition of carpets from China. These carpets are of very high quality.

In preparation for the holiday season, we have special offers on suitcases. You will find these on the ground floor, at the back of the building.

When you go to the second floor, don't miss the music department which is at the top of the stairs, to the right. It has all the latest recordings from your favourite performers, on records, cassettes and compact discs. And opposite that, there's the bookshop, which also stocks children's books and magazines.

On the third floor, next to the toy department, there's a special offer on tennis rackets, which are all reduced by ten per cent today only. Make sure you buy your new racket today.

(Pause) *Now listen again.*

(Repeat recording.)

That is the end of Part 3.

You now have a minute to check your answers. We will tell you when Part 4 begins.

Part 4 (page 106)

Now turn to Part 4, questions 20 to 25.
*Look at the six statements for this Part. You will hear a conversation between a man and a woman. Decide if you think each statement is correct or incorrect. If you think it is correct, put a tick in the box under **A**. If you think it is not correct, put a tick in the box under **B**. At the end the recording is repeated.*

(Pause) *Now we are ready to start. Listen carefully.*

Man   Have you got the shopping list?
Woman   Yes. Here it is. Let me see ... fruit, vegetables, cheese, meat, paint ...
Man   Let's go and get the paint first. I think the shop opposite the bus station would be best. There's a car park in the next street.

Woman   Just a minute. I think we should go to the butcher's first. Or to the supermarket. Those shops get so crowded later on. And then we can get the vegetables in the market. We can pick up the paint on the way home.
Man   It'll probably take ages to choose the paint.
Woman   What do you mean? I thought we'd decided to get cream.
Man   Well ... I'm not sure about the colour.
Woman   I thought we'd discussed all that last night. I thought you said you wanted cream.
Man   No, I didn't. I didn't say I definitely wanted cream. And now I think about it, I'm not at all sure that cream would be the right colour. I think we should look at some of the other colours before we decide.
Woman   But we're going to start painting this afternoon.
Man   That's all right.
Woman   No, it isn't ... if we're going to spend all day arguing about colours. And there's the rest of the shopping to be done.
Man   Well, you get the other things, and I'll choose the paint.
Woman   Oh no. You might choose a colour I don't like. I suppose we'd better go and choose the paint first. If it takes too long, we can forget about shopping for food and you can take me out to a restaurant for dinner.
Man   All right.

(Pause) *Now listen again.*

(Repeat recording.)

That is the end of Part 4. You now have twelve minutes to check and transfer your answers to the Answer Sheet.